Praise for
Marketing in the Moment

"Michael's 3.0 marketing strategies took my business from a dying brick and mortar company to a profitable online money-making machine. I've reduced overhead and increased profit while spending more time with my family and less time in my business!"

—**Matthew Ferry**, bestselling author of *Creating Sales Velocity*, the "Players' Coach," www.matthewferry.com

"I highly recommend this book! It is a must-read for anyone wanting to learn from one of the top marketing minds in the world!"

—**Bill Bartmann**, self-made billionaire and two-time National Entrepreneur of the Year, Founder of Billionaire Business Systems

"Want to get ahead of your competition, fast? Then read *Marketing in the Moment*. Tasner's strategies focus on the future of online marketing, Web 3.0. This is innovative and forward-thinking material that is also practical and easy to use. Tasner has written the perfect desk reference for any online marketer!"

—**Joel Comm**, *New York Times* bestselling author of *Twitter Power*

"Forget asking your teenager or your computer geek how to navigate Web changes that keep coming at us faster and faster. They may know what button to push, but they know nothing about how to adapt marketing to keep up with these changes! *Marketing in the Moment* replaced my fear of the unknown in this rapidly changing online marketing environment and replaced it with security that I can actually know what I need in order to make the very best marketing decisions to boost my company profits. As a 25-year-old successful entrepreneur, Michael Tasner brings us his generation's unique know-how and ease of adaptability in the ever-shifting sands of new technology, and as a successful marketing expert he explains exactly what I need to do with my marketing to make it work in this environment."

—**Amy Levinson**, MPA, Executive Vice President, Guerrilla Marketing International, www.gmarketing.com

"If you want to make serious money online using the *latest* strategies, you've got to devour Michael Tasner's hot new book called *Marketing in the Moment*. I loved it!"

—**Robert G. Allen**, author of the bestsellers *Multiple Streams of Income, Multiple Streams of Internet Income, The One Minute Millionaire, Creating Wealth*, and *Cash in a Flash: Fast Money in Slow Times*

"If you cannot generate money online after implementing the realistic insights and strategies revealed in Tasner's book, *Marketing in the Moment*, then throw in the towel—game over!"

—**Joel Bauer**, author, speaker, and mentor

"After reading *Marketing in the Moment* I wondered how my life may be different if I had this knowledge even a year ago. I would have saved time, money, and effort. The information is concise, timely, and effective."

—**Dr. John Spencer Ellis**, CEO, National Exercise & Sports Trainers Association; creator of the movie *The Compass*

"With the rapid change for marketers and businesses, knowing the right thing to do is a must! It's do or die. *Marketing in the Moment* gives the reader the right tools to win and now!"

—**Jeffrey Hayzlett**, author of *The Mirror Test*; Chief Marketing Officer, Kodak

"The online marketing world is changing fast and nobody knows for sure what's coming next. This book can help you be better prepared for the changes that are already afoot."

—**Tony Hsieh**, author of *Delivering Happiness*; CEO, Zappos

"As a publicity coach and publicity thought leader, I can safely say that this book is definitely an online marketing wake-up call! Web 2.0 is out, Web 3.0 is in! One of the many things I loved about this book is that Tasner provides you real-world examples of all the strategies he talks about. His in-depth descriptions are easy to follow and understand, so you can take them and implement them in your own business."

—**Dan Janal**, Founder, PR LEADS, www.prleadsplus.com

"Michael Tasner is a pioneer in sharing the inside secrets of the next generation of online marketing—also known as Web 3.0 marketing. If you read this book, you'll be ahead of the curve and get a lead on your competitors. If not, your marketing will become obsolete."

—**Manny Goldman**, CEO, Personal Growth Marketing; Founder, PersonalGrowth.com

"*Marketing in the Moment* oozes with opportunity. It's filled with powerful, profitable, and practical ideas on using Web 3.0 technology to take your business to the next level. Get started today."

—**Jill Konrath**, bestselling author of *SNAP Selling* and *Selling to Big Companies*

"Michael Tasner, with his on-target book, *Marketing in the Moment*, has gotten in front of the wave with present marketing trends. We are an 'I want it now' society. The book is easy to read and navigate, with numerous valuable resources. I love the Case Studies and Checklists, but the To Do lists are worth a million bucks! If you want to dominate your niche in today's market, you need this book!"

—**Robby LeBlanc**, www.MarketingYouCanUse.com

"Michael's book is right on target. What I love most about the book are the step-by-step instructions. Too many marketing books are filled with theory, and this one is all meat. If you want to sell more products or services online, you need this one right away!"

—**Ryan Lee**, entrepreneur, author, coach, www.ryanlee.com

"When I first met Michael Tasner, I instantly knew he was qualified to write this book. Why? Because of his unique business card that stood out from the crowd of about 40 others that I met that day. He practices what he preaches. This book is easy to read, well explained, and most of all, practical. Buy it, take action with the enclosed To Do's, and I know you'll profit."

—**Andrew Lock**, www.HelpMyBusiness.com, the #1 WebTV show for entrepreneurs

"Think you know it all about online marketing? Then read *Marketing in the Moment* and be blown away by the future of the Internet, Web 3.0! Michael Tasner is a leading marketing expert who delivers this ingenious guide to online marketing. I know that this book is full of strategies that will get you ahead of the competition and make you more money."

—**Eric Lofholm**, author of *How to Sell in the New Economy*

"I highly recommend this book! It is a must-read for anyone wanting to learn from one of top marketing minds in the world!"

—**Jill Lublin**, international speaker and bestselling author

"I am of the belief that *everything* is shifting. That the paradigm within which we've been operating, in business specifically, has gone bankrupt. That the way we've done things up until now—the way we've created, marketed, and distributed content; the way we've communicated with our partners, vendors, and customers; the mindset behind delivering our bottom line; and every other component in how we do business—has actually expired and a new model is emerging.

"As a huge believer that this twenty-first century shift in business is grounded and founded in collaboration and contribution, I was thrilled beyond measure to see that these are two concepts Tasner points to in *Marketing in the Moment*.

"I know that where we're going to start seeing this shift evidenced loudly is in the world of marketing. Tasner may be talking about Web 3.0, but what he's actually doing is *exemplifying* this twenty-first century shift in business.

"The content he provides is rich and exceedingly helpful in taking readers by the hand and crossing them over the bridge as we make this transition into the new paradigm for doing business. The most powerful piece for me, however, is in witnessing Tasner as an actual demonstration of what twenty-first century business is all about.

"I know *Marketing in the Moment* will prove to be a manual for those of us seeking support as we forge forward even further into this digital age."

—**Liora Mendeloff**, CEO and Founder, InstantMediaKit.com

"Michael Tasner has unlocked the vault to his multimillion dollar mind and given you *everything* you need to be successful on the Web today! Rarely does someone of Michael's stature reveal such profound secrets (the secrets he uses to run his own business!), and if that weren't enough, he also makes it so simple to follow his lead and execute his strategies. He's really taken the complexity out of it. If you want to succeed on the Web today, whether you want to do it yourself or you just want to disqualify 90% of the 'Web designers' out there who want to 'help' you, this is the book for you. This book is an absolute *must*-read."

—**Nick Nanton**, Esq., "The Celebrity Lawyer," www.DicksNanton.com

"*Marketing in the Moment* is a must-read for any marketer or business professional! Tasner divulges amazing strategies, tips, and ideas that will push you to the forefront of online marketing. Not only is the information critical to stay ahead of the competition, but he lays it out in a practical, easy-to-use format. This book is an amazing guide for anyone, from marketing novices to experienced veterans!"

—**Ed Oakley**, Founder and CEO, Enlightened Leadership Solutions, Inc.

"Folks, do buy this book and read it immediately. Web 2.0 is over-saturated and dying. Web 3.0 is where you should be. It's targeted and does not soak up your time. Tasner shows you exactly what it is and how you can take advantage of it. Super information and simply written."

—**Srikumar S. Rao**, author of *Happiness at Work: Be Resilient, Motivated and Successful—No Matter What*, TED speaker

"There is a ton of stuff written about Web 2.0 marketing but very little about Web 3.0 marketing. This book changes that completely. If you are looking to grab some low-hanging fruit, now is the time using Tasner's tactics!"

—**Freddie Rick**, Founder, BetterTrades

"When it comes to marketing on the Web, it's not just advisable to keep up with the trends, it's essential. Where and how people seek out information continues to change, and the key to successful marketing is to identify what's happening and adapt early on.

"If you don't reach your customers first, someone else will.

"In this no-nonsense, easy-to-read guide, Michael Tasner breaks down today's top emerging marketplaces, devices, and technology to help your business stay one step ahead.

"You'll learn what to look for, how to take action, and most importantly, how to get results. You'll master Web 3.0 marketing before your competitors have Facebook figured out."

—**David Rivers**, President, KegWorks.com

"Put on your seat-belt...if propelling your personal brand or corporate brand is a goal or challenge on your dashboard. Michael Tasner's *Marketing in the Moment* is a must in the equation of Web 3.0 success."

—**Kenneth J. Skiba**, Sales Leader & CEO, YouHaveGotToBeKidding.com

"Web 2.0 is old news—Web 3.0 is in! Tasner unleashes his marketing expertise to educate you on the future of online marketing. *Marketing in the Moment* is an easy-to-use guide for any business professional, marketer, or sales person who wants to be ahead of the competition and make more money. If that sounds good to you, then you need to read this book."

—**Melanie Benson Strick**, CEO, Success Connections, Inc., www.successconnections.com

"Why go to an expensive Internet marketing course when everything you need for Web 3.0 is right here in Michael Tasner's excellent book *Marketing in the Moment*? With Internet marketing growing by leaps and bounds, it might seem difficult to keep up. But after reading Tasner's book, learning his many easy-to-learn practical strategies, I'm ready to conquer the Internet. I strongly recommend this book."

—**Joseph Sugarman**, Chairman, BluBlocker Corporation; author of *Advertising Secrets of the Written Word*

"Michael Tasner's new book will rock your world! He shares and teaches absolutely the most current, cutting edge strategies to successfully market your product or business on the Internet. If you are in business and you are online, you need this book."

—**Dan Thurmon**, author of *Off Balance On Purpose*

"This powerful book is loaded with great ideas to help you attract more customers and make more sales—immediately!"

—**Brian Tracy**, author of *The Art of Closing the Sale*

"'In the moment' means having a connection with your customers and marketing with authenticity. In this book, Tasner lays out a plan any business owner or sales professional can use to connect authentically in a way never before possible. Chapter 6 alone is worth the price of the entire book. Buy it or be left behind."

—**Jimmy Vee and Travis Miller**, bestselling authors of *Gravitational Marketing: The Science of Attracting Customers,* Founders of GravitationalMarketing.com

Marketing in the Moment

Marketing in the Moment

The Practical Guide to Using Web 3.0 Marketing to Reach Your Customers First

Michael Tasner

FT Press offers excellent discounts on this book when ordered in quantity for bulk purchases or special sales. For more information, please contact U.S. Corporate and Government Sales, 1-800-382-3419, corpsales@pearson-techgroup.com. For sales outside the U.S., please contact International Sales at international@pearson.com.

Company and product names mentioned herein are the trademarks or registered trademarks of their respective owners.

Pearson Education LTD.
Pearson Education Australia PTY, Limited
Pearson Education Singapore, Pte. Ltd.
Pearson Education North Asia, Ltd.
Pearson Education Canada, Ltd.
Pearson Educación de Mexico, S.A. de C.V.
Pearson Education—Japan
Pearson Education Malaysia, Pte. Ltd.

Library of Congress Cataloging-in-Publication Data

Tasner, Michael Scott, 1984–
    Marketing in the moment : the practical guide to using Web 3.0 marketing to reach your customers first / Michael Tasner. — 1st ed.
        p. cm.
    Includes index.
    ISBN 978-0-13-708109-7 (hardback : alk. paper) 1. Internet marketing. 2. Web 3.0. I. Title.
    HF5415.1265T37 2010
    658.8'72—dc22
                                        2010006095

Vice President, Publisher
Tim Moore

Associate Publisher and Director of Marketing
Amy Neidlinger

Acquisitions Editors
Megan Colvin
Jennifer Simon

Editorial Assistants
Myesha Graham
Pamela Boland

Development Editor
Russ Hall

Operations Manager
Gina Kanouse

Senior Marketing Manager
Julie Phifer

Publicity Manager
Laura Czaja

Assistant Marketing Manager
Megan Colvin

Cover Designer
Chuti Prasertsith

Managing Editor
Kristy Hart

Project Editor
Betsy Harris

Copy Editor
Cheri Clark

Proofreader
Water Crest Publishing

Indexer
Lisa Stumpf

Compositor
Nonie Ratcliff

Manufacturing Buyer
Dan Uhrig

Icon Illustrations
istockphoto

To my beautiful wife, Anna, and my handsome twin boys, Connor and Logan.

Table of Contents

Foreword

If you're a guerrilla marketer, online and mobile marketing were invented for you. Why? Guerrilla marketers recognize the power of custom-tailored marketing. They know how important is to be fast on their feet, changing quickly to reflect everything they learn about their customers. Above all, they know how important it is to squeeze maximum bang out of every buck. Today's online and mobile channels are perfect for all that. They can help you transform marketing squirt guns into cannons—*if* you know what you're doing.

That's where this book comes in.

Forget the hype and hand-waving that won't earn you a single customer or sale. Michael Tasner gets down to brass tacks: proven tactics and ground-level execution techniques. He shows you *what* you need to do. *How* and *when* to do it. What *works*. And what *doesn't* work—no matter how much money you throw at it or how many breathless, bill-by-the-hour experts tell you otherwise.

What gives Tasner the right to write this book? Only this: He's been doing it for a decade. *Really* doing it. Through booms and busts alike, he's built one of the nation's leading online marketing firms. He's guided companies of all kinds, from Internet startups to *nine* Fortune® 1000 companies. And, as a certified Guerrilla Marketing Master Trainer, he knows how to assess the terrain, recognize and act on new opportunities fast, and defeat even the most well-armed competitors.

You've got limited resources—maybe more limited than usual these days. Tasner walks you through prioritizing those resources for maximum impact. He helps you craft focused action plans for the next three, six, and twelve months—and offers specific guidance for meeting most any goal you have, including entering new markets.

Once your plan's in place, you must get your whole team on the same page fast so you can execute quickly, without bureaucracy or overhead. New online collaboration tools can help you do that. Tasner shows you how to use them *at practically no cost*.

Maybe you're looking around at all those smartphone and iPad users, and you're salivating. If you're not, you should be. Practically overnight, mobile's become as endemic as phones and computers. You're thinking: There's *got* to be a marketing opportunity here—but *where*? For most entrepreneurs and marketers, mobile is a mystery. It needn't be. Tasner shows you how to pick your spots and get started, with surprisingly little risk or investment.

Which brings me to another great thing about *Marketing in the Moment*. Unlike entrepreneurs and businesspeople who fail, savvy guerrilla marketers *know* they don't know everything. Guerrilla marketers ask questions: plenty of them. This book answers those questions: about everything from Twitter to iPhones. Guerrilla marketers want to learn from other people's costly mistakes, instead of reproducing them. This book draws giant fluorescent glow-in-the-dark circles around the money pits and sinkholes you *don't* want to fall into.

As I've long stressed, technology helps with the job—but it doesn't *do* the job. That was true of email and the Web: It's equally true with Facebook and Twitter. The job is still yours. *You* need to comprehend what the technology can and can't do for you—and then *you* need to execute. *You* need to measure what you're doing, learn from your customers, fix problems, do better.

Above all, *you* need to make the decision to get started, and grab these new online and mobile marketing opportunities before your competitors do. When you make that decision, you'll need resources to help you follow up with smarter choices, more effective execution, and fewer missteps. Fortunately, there's now a book you can rely on for all of that: Michael Tasner's *Marketing in the Moment*.

—Jay Conrad Levinson

Author and creator of *Guerrilla Marketing*, the world's most powerful approach to marketing, with 21,000,000 books sold in 62 languages

Acknowledgments

This was such a fun journey! I didn't realize all the hard work that actually went into making a book of this caliber.

First off, I want to thank my family: all of my parents, my brothers and sisters, my grandparents, and my aunts and uncles. All of you have provided so much support and encouragement over the years. You let me know that anything is possible when you put your mind to it. I hope that I, too, have been an inspiration back to you.

Thanks also to everyone at my company, Taz Solutions, who had a hand in the editing process. You all rock! In addition, I want to thank my clients; it's been an honor to serve you and help with your online marketing. Many times, you have let me make you my "guinea pigs," and I'm grateful you trusted me to lead the way. I was able to use many of you as case studies in the book, so thank you for allowing me to do that.

I want to give a special thanks to Martha Finney. You were an amazing editor and the reason I went with FT Press. I owe quite a bit to you.

Lastly, this book would not have been possible without the amazing support from FT Press. It was been a pleasure and an honor to get to work with such a talented team of people!

I am ever grateful for this book; it's truly a dream come true.

About the Author

Michael Tasner has been called by many as one of the top online marketing experts in the world. He runs a large online marketing and design firm that works with the most high-profile speakers, authors, consultants, and entrepreneurs in the world. These businesses hire and trust him to run their entire online marketing campaigns from A to Z. He has also consulted with numerous Fortune 1000 companies, teaching them how to implement the latest and greatest Web efforts in their marketing.

The best part: He plays both sides of the fence. Not only does he run Taz Solutions, Inc., but he trains others how to market on their own. His experience is backed by more than ten years of in-the-trenches work. During those ten years, he has started and sold four successful Web firms based on the traffic they were generating.

Michael lives in Niagara Falls, NY with his wife, Anna, and twin boys, Connor and Logan.

Introduction

There has never been a better time in history than now to be marketing on the Internet. Look around at some of the retail giants that have gone out of business or filed for bankruptcy recently: Circuit City, Steve & Barry's, Linens 'n Things, Shoe Pavilion, and Whitehall Jewelry. Now compare them to similar online businesses: www.Amazon.com, www.Zappos.com, www.MyWeddingFavors.com, and www.BlueNile.com.

Both consumers and businesses have shifted the way they purchase products and services, but more important, they have shifted the way they research and find these products and services. This is where we as marketers need to focus our attention. We need to be certain that we are marketing in the right places, or we can start saying goodbye to business. What did the online companies do differently than the retail ones? They understood and embraced a move that was taking place in the marketing world.

How would you like to be ahead of 98% of other marketers, gain an unfair advantage over your competitors, and start grabbing market share before anyone realizes they should have been doing the same for the past year?

Hopefully, you answered yes. I mean, who wouldn't want to be on the leading edge and grabbing market share before all the rest do? Before we tell how this is going to happen, let's take a step back and put some things into perspective.

Recognize Any of These?

Sit back for a second and think about this first set of terms:

> *collaboration, blogging, content sharing, online video, social networks*

Now think about this second set of terms:

> *mobile browsing, live streaming video, microblogging, personalization, semantic*

Let's try one more exercise: Take a look at these two groups of companies. How many are you familiar with in each group?

> **Group 1:** Facebook, Wikipedia, Blogger, YouTube, PRWeb, Squidoo, TypePad, MySpace, Scribd
>
> **Group 2:** Twitter, Plurk, Ustream, Joost, Tumblr, iGoogle, OpenID, Salesforce, Funsites

Chances are you recognize many more in the first group than in the second. The good news: You're in the majority. The bad news: Time is of the essence.

The purpose of these two exercises was to show you the different trends that are already taking place and the new companies that are shaping the future of the Web. In the first exercise, *collaboration, blogging, content sharing, online video,* and *social networks* all are Web 2.0 terms. The second group was composed of Web 3.0 terms. In the second exercise, group 1 is composed of Web 2.0 companies, and group 2 is composed of Web 3.0 companies. Rather than clouding your judgment with preconceived notions, we wanted you to see the shift for yourself.

Many people have said we are still years away from Web 3.0. We reply, we are already living it. The drastic shift is already taking place with changes happening all around us. We have been so encapsulated with Web 2.0 that we have put blinders on to the shift to Web 3.0.

What Does This Mean to You?

In uncertain economic times, we cannot ignore trends. We need to learn about and start capitalizing on them. You must be certain that you are bringing in customers from various sources—sources from which your target audience is based. The old days of consumers and businesses simply going to Google, typing in a search phrase, locating a company, and purchasing are over with. They are watching live presentations on Ustream, getting 140-character posts on Twitter with special offers, and even browsing Second Life to learn more. They also have most likely browsed your Web site from a device other than a computer, whether it was a BlackBerry, an iPhone, or another mobile device. Are you prepared to embrace and leverage these changes?

Move Out of the Way, or Jump on the Bullet Train

Marketing in the Moment is meant to serve as your step-by-step guidebook to allowing you to make the shift from a Web 2.0 marketing world to a Web 3.0 marketing universe. If you're not ready to be on the forefront of the marketing world, this book is not for you. However, if you are ready to establish your "Blue Ocean Strategy" (book by W. Chan Kim and Renee Mauborgne), then let's dive in and start breaking you away from the pack. Trust me, Web 3.0 is where you want to be!

Why Should You Listen to Me?

I run a large online marketing and design firm that works with the most high-profile speakers, authors, consultants, and entrepreneurs in the world. These businesses hire us and trust us to run their entire online marketing campaigns from A to Z. I've also consulted with numerous Fortune 1000 companies, teaching them how to implement the latest and greatest Web efforts in their marketing.

The best part: I play both sides of the fence. Not only do I run Taz Solutions, Inc., where we do the marketing for you, but I train others (like you) how to do this on your own. My experience is backed by over ten years of in-the-trenches work. During those ten years, I've started and sold four successful Web firms based on the traffic they were generating.

At 25, I've been called one of the top marketing experts in the world. This is a very interesting title to have at such a young age. I've been called this for one simple reason: I produce results that others have only dreamed of.

How to Use This Book

I want this to be your desk reference to Web 3.0 marketing. Read the book from cover to cover at least twice. This was written as a tactical book for a reason. One of the biggest complaints I get from people is that they don't know how to implement. They read plenty of "feel good" and strategy stuff, but most of those books are light on implementation. Take the famous movie *The Secret*. The movie was life-changing, but nowhere did it tell you how to actually start seeing some of the changes come into your day-to-day life. What I'm getting at here is this: There are no excuses as to why you can't implement this stuff. It's not too hard, and it's been boiled down for you.

Throughout the book, you will see some different symbols. Here are their meanings:

Checklist

You will find a variety of checklists and lists in general. These are there for your reference.

To Do

This book is light on fluff and heavy on tactics that will get you results. We will be talking about how to leverage certain marketing tactics. Under the To Do icon, you will see a boiled-down list of action items for you to start implementing in ten steps or fewer.

Case Study

For each of the major marketing tactics we are teaching you about, a case study of how that tactic has been used in real life is included. Also included with the case study is the key result achieved from the tactic and the takeaway I want you to get.

Tas Tip

Tas Tips are the "ah-ha" points throughout the book.

FAQs

Before we get started, let's tackle some of the most frequently asked questions.

Do All the Tactics Apply to My Business?

The simple answer: no. Keep in mind that most tactics will apply, even if you don't see it at first. Take, for example, the chapter on virtual reality worlds. It may sound far-fetched for you to use a virtual reality world to drive business or leads, but when you actually take a step back, it may not seem so ridiculous. Read over the case studies. Some of the more unique case studies were added to allow you to see the wide range of uses.

Is Web 3.0 Marketing Expensive to Do?

Most of the Web 3.0 tactics we will be discussing are very low-cost but high-impact. Effective marketing does not necessarily mean that it needs to be costly. It does, however, need to produce results and have the ability to be tracked and then tweaked.

Who Does This Book Apply To?

Entrepreneurs, speakers, authors, consultants, home-based businesses, corporations looking to gain an edge, infopreneurs, and intrapreneurs can all benefit from this book.

Are There Other Tools in This Book Besides Online Marketing?

There are a ton of resources in this book for both offline and online use. Throughout the book, there is also a variety of practical, no-BS, business advice on general marketing. Plain and simple, I want your business to succeed. Leveraging innovative marketing tactics to increase your traffic and leads is simply one route to get you there quickly.

1

The Mindset Shift: From Web 2.0 to Web 3.0

What Is Web 2.0?

Web 2.0 began when Web users started to drastically change the way they were using the Web on a day-to-day basis. The main trends that shaped Web 2.0 include content sharing, creativity, segmentation, social components, and added functionality. Some of the added functionality is peer-to-peer sharing of files, easier communication and networking on various social marketing sites, video sharing, and blogging. Web directories evolved to social tagging, personal Web sites shifted to blogs, and online versions of encyclopedias morphed into Wikipedia. In the Web 2.0 world, collaborating on social networks and sharing information helped shape the trend relatively quickly.

As a marketing advantage, there are four key components to Web 2.0:

- **Social networks** are the sites where people come together and share ideas, thoughts, and comments. Examples: Facebook, LinkedIn, and MySpace.

- **Social media** are the places where you can share content with the world in hopes of spreading awareness. Examples: YouTube, Scribd, and Flickr.

- **User-generated content** was what sparked much of the discussion on Web 2.0. This is where users create, manage, and update information. Examples: Squidoo, blogs, and Wikipedia.

- **Social news and bookmarking** have allowed users to organize their Web experience. Examples: Digg, Delicious, and StumbleUpon.

The Limitations of Web 2.0

For many people, Web 2.0 is the king of the mountain. On the contrary, I want to rip it apart, tear it to shreds, and show you all the loopholes, which, in turn, become fresh opportunities.

There are five essential limiting factors of Web 2.0:

- Oversaturation
- Misconceptions
- Time
- Modes of Interaction
- Openness

Oversaturation

Let's start with the limiting factor that should command the most attention: oversaturation. The problem is that everyone and their third cousin are on the Web 2.0 bandwagon.

As a society, we have become so obsessed with Web 2.0 that it has become *oversaturated*! All of this saturation causes an exorbitant amount of unnecessary noise.

Key Concept:

The key limitation to Web 2.0 is that it has become oversaturated.

Here are some examples:

- Your grandma calls you and says she's been told she needs a blog so that her friends can stay updated on her travels.
- Eight-year-olds are posting videos on YouTube.
- Photos of your kid's birthday are shared with the world on Flickr.

You might argue that, as a result, these sites are receiving a lot of good traffic because everyone is logging on. You are correct. However, how *targeted* is the traffic going to be? This is a key concept you will hear throughout the book. Targeted traffic is the advantage that strategic marketers are seeking.

When it comes down to it, the key is drilling down to find the best interaction. Facebook is an excellent place to network, meet new people, and do business. But Facebook is a powerful marketing tool only when you know how to use it to reach out to specific people or groups of people.

Misconceptions

Common misconceptions about Web 2.0 have also caused difficulties. How many times have you heard that MySpace is just for teens and porn? The statement is nowhere near correct; however, there are millions of people who firmly hold that statement to be true. Those are the people who are very tough to reach using Web 2.0 marketing methods.

The media portray Web 2.0 in one way. The fact of the matter is that some people can ruin it for all of us. You get some crazy 14-year-old from China creating a virus, and suddenly everyone thinks that their computers are infected and that they can't open any attachments or even browse the Web.

Time

Time is also a limiting factor. As we become more and more connected, we get more and more distracted by all the noise, like comments being made on our blogs, questions about our photos on Flickr, or updates on Wikipedia. One trend that never seems to change is that people continue to get busier and have less time for interaction.

Both consumers and businesses continue to demand more information, and they want it faster, making it very challenging to keep up. Once they think they have found their preferred method of communication (e-mail), an even better method comes out that is even faster (to be talked about shortly).

Modes of Interaction

I understand that this way of thinking may be contradictory to what you might be thinking: Isn't the goal of Web 2.0 to create new modes of interaction? I define modes of interaction as the different places and devices that people use to gather, search, network, and exchange information. People are gathering in different places around the Web and interacting in different ways with each other. But these modes of interaction have decreased the human touch. Do you even pick up a phone on a daily basis? If you need something, you pop off an e-mail. If you have a question, you search Wikipedia.

Once you start getting bogged down with e-mails, Facebook messages, and instant messages, you start to look for a solution to simplify things, and a bad taste forms in your mouth. Then you reach the tipping point, making you jump ship and focus on something else. In other words, there is just too much out there, thus causing confusion and a lack of adoption.

Openness

Lastly, the openness of Web 2.0 has become a striking limitation. Most humans are naturally private. When you have a Facebook account, a MySpace account, and a Flickr page, your privacy drops quickly. If you are an avid user of Facebook or read the news, you will remember when Facebook changed their policy to state that they own your content even after you've canceled your account. They did change that policy back, but it's still quite vague in their favor. We enjoy sharing details about ourselves, but there comes a point where it just gets weird or creepy. Take, for example, Google Ads on Gmail. You actually will see ads based on the text phrases you're typing in your e-mail. So if you happen to write "personal development," you will see targeted ads with that phrase!

What Is Web 3.0 Marketing?

Web 3.0 marketing describes the next wave that is already taking place and is the shift from Web 2.0. The key driving factors to Web 3.0 marketing include browsing habits, browsing methods, more intelligent information, the experience we're looking for, and the openness of the Web. BlackBerrys and iPhones, portals into Web 3.0, are ruling the day. **Simplified:** Web 3.0 marketing is the convergence of new technologies and rapidly changing consumer buying trends.

Live, streaming video is outpacing static video, and companies like Twitter, Plurk, and Jaiku are growing much more rapidly than Blogger, WordPress, or TypePad. The Web 3.0 marketing world is where customized, intelligent information is available at our fingertips, on any device, from anywhere in the world!

The Five Key Components of Web 3.0 Marketing

- **Microblogging** is the ability to share your thoughts with a set number of characters. People are busy with limited time, so why not get right to the point of the story in 140 characters or fewer? Examples include Twitter, Plurk, and Jaiku.

- **Virtual reality worlds** are places users visit to interact with others from around the world in a 3-D setting. Meetings are being conducted in these spaces, and trade shows are being replaced with virtual reality shows. Examples include Second Life and Funsites.

- **Customization/personalization** allows visitors to create a more personalized experience. They are starting to expect their name to appear at the top of Web sites, personal e-mails, and even advanced checkout options that suit their buying habits. As the Web becomes more and more intelligent, personalization will be the norm. Examples include SendOutCards, Google, and Amazon.

- **Mobile** plays on the fact that there are billions of cell-phone users throughout the world. This number is much larger than those that use PCs. Consumers are surfing the Web and purchasing products right from their mobile phones. They are also using their phones and becoming instant journalists by shooting raw footage of random acts. Examples include iPhones and BlackBerrys.

- **On-demand collaboration** allows users to interact in real time by looking over documents, collaborating, and making changes in real time. Software as a service also fits into on-demand collaboration as it allows users to leverage only Web-based solutions. Examples include Google Docs, www.Salesforce.com, www.Slideshare.net, and www.Box.net.

Let's review the limitations of Web 2.0 so you can see how these start fitting nicely into Web 3.0 marketing:

Web 2.0 Limitation	Web 3.0 Marketing Solution	Web 3.0 Marketing Tool
Oversaturation	It's just getting started.	All the Web 3.0 marketing tactics.
Misconceptions	People don't know enough about Web 3.0 to judge it yet.	All the Web 3.0 marketing tactics.
Time	Quicker and shorter.	Twitter, text messages.
Modes of Interaction	Live, cellphones.	Ustream, BlackBerry, iPhone.
Openness	Specialized, closed communities, less invasive.	InterNations, Pingsta, ASMALLWORLD.

2

Are You Ready for Web 3.0 Marketing?

How Web 3.0 Marketing Will Affect Your Business, Your Company, and Your Life

There are four key areas in which you're going to notice changes, as described next.

Increasing Mobility and Reliance on Mobile Devices

Mobile is the largest and fastest-growing Web 3.0 trend in online marketing!

BlackBerrys and iPhones are becoming the norm. Text messaging used to be the gold standard. Now, if you don't have e-mail and Web access, your phone is considered ancient. This trend will affect your personal life as well as your business life.

Resistance to Sharing Information with Everyone

The openness of the Web is causing some major issues with personal security. Identity theft is massively on the rise. In 2008, there were almost ten million victims, a 22% rise from 2007, along with incidences of viruses and spyware. Consumers and businesses are starting to get more skeptical about putting information on the Web as they become more aware of the *possible* repercussions.

Whatever you put out on the Web can be found, digested, and used by anyone. In fact, there have been recent cases of hackers using the Web to rummage around in your hard drive and even to turn your own monitor against you, remotely activating your webcam and watching what's going on in your office.

In addition to the technical protections people are installing—not to mention the strict rules of online conduct they're imposing on their workplaces and families—there is a trend of microcommunity sites and tribes, as Seth Godin calls them in *Tribes: We Need You to Lead Us*. Facebook will not become a thing of the past, but smaller, more central- ized, and specialized groups and social sites will become more prevalent. As a marketer, you will need to establish a presence on these sites so that people can get to know, like, and trust you.

A Reduction in the Need to Be "Belly-to-Belly"

There are many reasons people are continuing to flock to the Web for virtual communication instead of jumping on a plane for a face-to-face meeting, with the largest reason being cost. It is very expensive to fly across the country, stay in a hotel, dine out, take taxis, and on top of it all miss both work and, more important, family time. Virtual trade shows are gaining in popularity. www.SecondLife.com continues to get larger, and services like www.GoToMeeting and www.WebEx.com are attracting new customers like crazy. Citrix (which owns GoToMeeting) continues to attract more than 15,000 new users each month. WebEx touts more than 7 million worldwide users leveraging its tool each month.

Once you go virtual, you may never want to fly again, at least for a business meeting. Once you go cam-to-cam, face-to-face will never be the same!

Everything Is Continuing to Go to the Web

Anything and everything continues to go to the Web. Twelve-year-olds are running million-dollar social networks, pizza companies are taking orders through the Web, your family diner accepts reservations on the Net, your grandma is tweeting, your long-lost cousin runs a popular tribe on Second Life. And the list goes on, and on, and on. This trend will not change.

Conducting a 360-Degree Review of Your Web Platform and Marketing Efforts

I'm a huge fan of 360-degree reviews. You may have heard of these. They are typically used in the Human Resource department of a company for employee reviews. The objective of the review is to get a view from all different angles (thus the name 360 degrees) of the particular employee.

Here's how it works: You're an employee working at one of the large automakers (who will remain nameless). Assuming you still have a job, you work daily with other employees just like you, for a direct supervisor. And you have people reporting directly to you. In the process of conducting your review to decide whether you will get a two-cent-per-hour raise (I know, don't get too excited), your performance will be reviewed by your boss, your peers, and your own direct reports. This ensures that you're getting the most accurate representation of the quality of your work. It also serves as a great checks-and-balances system. If your boss didn't like you, that is only one leg of the review. And one of these days, you will be part of your boss's 360-degree review.

Let's take similar methodology and apply it to your current marketing tactics. This will allow us to see your greatest opportunities for expansion.

To Do

How to Conduct a 360-Degree Review of Your Web Efforts:

Step 1: *Make a list of all the people who have a hand in or are touched by your marketing efforts.*

For example: The CEO, your marketing director, marketing executives, salespeople, engineers, research and development folks, vendors, partners, and your customers. The key here is to make sure you are not leaving anyone out. If you miss one person, you are not fully getting a 360-degree review. You might get only 300 degrees.

Step 2: *Construct two to three surveys for those people to complete.*

The first survey will go to all internal employees, the second to your vendors/partners, if applicable, and the last to your customers. It's up to you if you want to send this to all your customers. It depends highly on how many customers you have. If you're a smaller company, I recommend sending it to all your customers. If you're a larger company with thousands of customers, send it to enough clients to get a good response back. Typical response rates range from 3% to 10%. I've seen lower,

but I've also seen response rates as high as 90%. But
those are just the averages.

A few important notes on these surveys:

- I encourage you to send these 100% electronically.
  When sending surveys electronically, you have a
  much higher chance of getting a response. There
  are various survey tools out there, such as
  www.SurveyMonkey.com, www.Zoomerang.com,
  and www.keysurvey.com.

- Keep them short to increase your response rate.

- Give some type of incentive for your outside vendors, partners, or customers to fill these out, and
  watch your response rates skyrocket. (For example,
  give them 10% off their next order.)

- Modify anything to fit your business.

I like allowing for comments after each question to
solicit additional feedback. The reason I ask and solicit
more open-ended feedback is to ensure that we don't
miss any of the trends. If your customers are finding you
in the underwater basket-weaving forum, and we don't
leave open space for them to fill in that info, we will
never discover that valuable information.

**To get these forms in an editable format, visit
www.marketinginthemomentbook.com/360.**

Step 3: *Compile the data.*

This is going to take you quite a bit of time. Here are
some tips for compiling the data:

- Many of the survey software tools will do this
  for you.

- Develop three different Microsoft Excel files and
  label them appropriately (internal, vendors/part-
  ners, customers).

- Start with the quantifiable data and get that into Excel. Most likely this will be a simple export.

- Move on to the open-ended questions. Take all the responses for each question and place them into Excel so you can see all the data in front of you.

- Scroll down the column of open-ended questions and look for trends. I like to use the find feature in Excel to see whether similar words are being found. For example, you could search for craigslist to see all the places it was mentioned.

- When you find similar answers in the open-ended questions, group those together.

- When you have this task done, you should be able to easily see the results for the quantifiable section, and all the answers to the open-ended sections grouped together with similar thoughts.

- Lastly, do the same thing with the comments as you did with the open-ended questions: Group similar comments together, using the find feature to aid in this task.

Step 4: *Interpret the data.*

You now have your data organized in a much more logical format so that you can start figuring out what it all means. Print out all the sheets and spread them out across a long desk so you can see everything. What you're looking for here are trends across the various groups, as well as weaknesses in your marketing strategy. Keep in mind that in this exercise, bad news is actually good—it's what you're looking for. It's great to see the good stuff, but we're more concerned with the areas in which you need to improve because these are your greatest opportunities for growth. What you are most likely going to find is two-fold:

First, 20% of your marketing is producing the most results. The other 80% is a waste of time, money, and energy.

Second, there are many new trends and places you can start leveraging in your online marketing strategy.

Case Study

When my team at Taz Solutions, Inc., was looking for ways to generate some new business, we turned to a 360-degree survey format. We interviewed our employees, contractors, vendors, and 650 of our customers to solicit targeted feedback. Because we were offering a $10,000 Web site makeover to one lucky winner, the customer response rate on the survey was upwards of 80%. Plain and simple, we got some solid feedback that allowed us to make the most informed and strategic decisions.

Google AdWords was proving to be a waste of money, whereas specialized Web forums were producing more qualified leads. But we were spending 70% of our own marketing budget on Google and less than 2% on marketing in forums. Obviously, something needed to change.

We also found that our prospects needed to be much more educated before being able to make the right decision.

The Result: We shifted our online marketing to make sure we were reaching entrepreneurs and business owners where they were searching and wanted to be reached. We also shifted from being overtly sales oriented to educating and serving our prospects first!

Our business continues to grow at a pace of over 100% a year, while most of our competitors are losing business or scaling back.

You can visit www.marketinginthemomentbook.com/360 for the full 360-degree review we looked at.

Step 5: *Compile your action plan, and continue reading this book!*

When you were going through all the data, I guarantee that your results came back pretty positive, but there were also several places you can start capitalizing on your added insights. You are going to hear about Twitter, mobile marketing, Second Life, new communities/forums, webinars, live videos, and so on. The whole point of doing the 360-degree review is to give you the starting point that applies to your business. Every business is different. Not every marketing method is going to be right for your business, but some of them will. Armed with internal and external data, you can make the best decisions about how to move forward in your Web 3.0 marketing plans.

Investing in New and Additional Technology

The good thing about Web 3.0 marketing is that there really are not a lot of expensive devices or systems I'd recommend you purchase. The key in Web 3.0 marketing technology is that you always want to steer yourself to Web-based solutions. Even the software itself is available as Web-based applications. Don't go purchasing any chunky devices that seem to be the new best thing, because chances are the same system is available 100% Web-based at one-tenth of the cost.

To get Web 3.0 marketing ready, you'll need a basic tool kit of some technology and talent. Here are the fundamentals that we recommend you start adopting and implementing in your organization:

- A system to send voice broadcasts to mobile phones, and one that will also send SMS (text messages). I recommend Trumpia (www.trumpia.com).

- A Web-based customer relationship management system. My favorite is Salesforce.com.

- An all-in-one solution for capturing leads, managing sales, and garnering affiliates. www.amazingshoppingcart.com is a great place to start.

- A solid team (or individual, to start), whether in-house or outsourced, that knows programming. This person should be able to develop applications, be able to work with open-source code, and ideally know how to program in Second Life. Check out www.RentACoder.com for ideas.

- A platform to virtually communicate and collaborate across a company. My all-time favorite company is Google. For instance, Taz Solutions, Inc., is a 100% virtual company. We have people working for the company across the globe, all from the comfort of their own homes. The biggest thing I realized from day one was that people love working from home, but if we didn't have solid systems in place to ensure their success, the company would be doomed before its first birthday.

Check out these Google apps:

- Gmail
- Google Docs
- Google Forms
- Google Chat (including video)
- Google Calendars

We'll get back to discussing collaboration in Chapter 9, "Collaboration: Connecting and Sharing Data at Lightning-Speed Paces."

The Top Five Things You Need to Do to Master and Prepare for the Web 3.0 Wave

To recap, here's what you need to do:

- Recognize that times are changing and trends are shifting.
- Conduct a 360-degree online-marketing review to solicit feedback.
- Take the feedback to heart, and start implementing the changes.
- Invest in some new technology.
- Capitalize on and grab market share while everyone else is still in denial.

3

Content Marketing: Understanding and Capitalizing on the Drastic Shift Taking Place

The Content-Delivery Change Taking Place

Have you ever heard the marketers' mantra that content is king? Here's an updated version of that idea: "Content is king on the Internet when delivered through the proper channels."

Over the past 12 months, there has been an enormous shift in the way content is being delivered and absorbed. To fully grasp the shift, take a look at what all the experts claim as one of the top ways to market your business: article submission. Submit a 500-plus-word article to Web sites like www.EzineArticles.com and to the various social-bookmarking sites, and expect to get amazing results very quickly.

www.EzineArticles.com is one of the largest online submission sites in the world. www.GoArticles.com is another.

The point of submitting content through these channels is twofold:

1. You get to include a signature file at the end of the article. These signature files are typically very keyword rich and aid in helping your search-engine ranking for that keyword over time.

2. You get some quality, organic traffic from people who read the article and want to learn more about you or your company.

These sites work only when what you have to say is directly interesting to the people you are targeting. Unless you're a celebrity, people aren't interested in what you have to say. They want to know how what you have to say benefits them. *Then* they'll be interested in what you have to say. And when they find something that pertains to them, they skim the information looking for the meat and the major facts to pull from.

As a society, we have less time to read long articles, even if they contain substantial information. *Time*—or rather the lack of it—is the driving factor in the content-delivery change. This lack of time is causing us as a society to turn to places and devices that give us what we're looking for quickly.

This lack of time has made way for two of the greatest Web 3.0 marketing methods, both of which have limited competition: sending information to mobile devices and microblogging, especially on Twitter.

From Blogging to Microblogging

Since this is a book about Web 3.0 marketing, I take blogging to another dimension and teach you about the trend that is already here; so if you don't have a blog, you have double the work to catch up on. Get a blog rocking, and then jump on the wave with the latest and greatest trend of microblogging. Keep reading. This is going to rock your world.

Blogging: What Is a Blog?

A blog is simply a Web site that is a compilation of ideas, thoughts, events, photos, or other content-based information that the author is interested in sharing. People started blogging in 1999 and, due to the ease of deployment and use, the relatively low cost, and the ability to reach a wide audience, they have been increasing in popularity ever since. Blogs are typically composed mainly of text content, but can and do include such elements as photos, videos, audio, and flash. Over 60% of the Web sites on the Internet today *still* do not have any type of blog. If you don't have a blog, you are missing out on traffic. Blogs are a great way of developing a following, starting a cultural trend or a political movement, establishing yourself as an expert, landing a book deal, and paying yourself through ad sales to indulge in your favorite expensive hobby. You can make a lot of money via blogs, either directly as companies recognize your site as a great place to advertise their own products and services, or indirectly as you become increasingly recognized as an expert and are paid for your advice or insights.

The top three blog systems are WordPress, Blogger, and TypePad. WordPress has the majority of the market share due to the vast amount of add-ons available. But Blogger and TypePad have been noted as easier to use and still maintain quite a few blogs on their servers.

The Two Key Types of Blogs

The two primary types of blogs are personal blogs and corporate/business blogs. There are other variations, but these are the main two that you see the most often:

- **Personal:** These blogs are the most popular in nature because they can be on any topic, including family, hobbies, sports, school, other interests, or even just emphatic opinions. It seems that people who post blogs on the Web ranting and raving about a product, a service, the latest movie, or someone in their social circle gain the most attention. Don't be afraid of offending readers—assuming, of course, that you believe in the opinion you're promoting. Let's face it: Controversy sells.

- **Corporate/Business:** Interested in promoting your products or services while building a relationship with your customers and prospects? Corporate blogs are a great tool for this task. Almost all the Fortune 1,000 companies maintain at least one public blog. The content typically is a mix between promotion of their offerings and some public relations content that is offered as a way to further build loyalty. This may range from photos of the executives having fun in the office, to customer testimonials, or even photos of employees' pets.

Other types of blogs include political, charity, media, and social blogs. One of my favorite other blog platforms is www.Squidoo.com. Squidoo is the brainchild of legendary marketer Seth Godin. On www.Squidoo.com, authors create what they refer to as "lens." These lens can be anything from how to cook great food to information about marketing on eBay. They currently have over 1,400,000 hand-built lenses!

Why Should You Be Blogging?

Blogs grow your visibility—and therefore enhance your marketing efforts. Search engines *LOVE* blogs because of their content-based nature.

Blogs are also one of the best places to start building (or expanding on) relationships. This should be considered an extension to your sales process. Most companies don't have enough resources to call on customers or prospects every day, but can easily "touch them" through this medium. Give them good content, and they will keep coming back for more. The notion that content is king on the Web stands and will continue to stand. The more original content you provide, the better. Good content provides readers with useful information.

How to Fully Utilize the Power of Your Blog

Many companies or individuals start blogs and update those only two or three times a month, if that. Your blog should be updated once *each and every single day*. The updates can be long articles with great information, a short sales pitch, a video, an audio, or even a photo.

I recommend that everyone utilize a blog as a marketing tool. The simple rationale: Google and the various search engines love blog content. Because of this, your blog will start ranking in the top of the search engines for different keywords and tags that you select for your content.

When most business leaders hear they should be updating their blog several times a day, they panic. This doesn't mean you need to log in and post every day. Get into the habit of batching your posts a few times each week and schedule them out to post in advance—a wonderful feature of blogging. Again, keep in mind that these posts do not always need to be long articles. It's best to provide useful content or tools to your blog readers, but random thoughts have also been well received. Frequency of posting is much more critical than the length of the content.

Get people excited about coming to your blog daily. You do that by blowing them away with amazing content and special offers just for them. Pepsi does a wonderful job at this by posting blog-only coupons for discounts on their products. www.Zappos.com offers blog readers access to a VIP area that provides guaranteed overnight shipping.

Since consumers have less and less time, keep your posts short and to the point. Your prospects are not going to read a 3,000-word blog post on your everyday thoughts. They will, however, read a post on the five things you need to know about creating a greener home, the three keys to a successful marriage, or the best five stocks to buy now and why. Keep your information tight, and you will maintain loyal readers.

Plug-ins/add-ons allow you to customize your blog. Some of the add-ons aid in providing technical help or details to remove spam and provide stats. Others help your readers stay in touch with you or follow you more easily. No blog can go without any plug-ins being used—they are just too powerful.

The current top plug-ins/add-ons include these:

- **SEO:** An amazing plug-in that makes your blog posts much more search-engine friendly.
- **Spam blocking:** A tool to help eliminate all the spam posts.
- **RSS feeds/feed burner:** A live RSS feed for anyone who prefers to use feeds to get their updates.
- **Twitter follower:** A direct link to Twitter.
- **Social tagging:** The ability for readers to tag the different blog posts.
- **Video customizer:** A tool that lets you customize your videos with ease.
- **Google sitemaps:** A tool to help Google index the blog more easily.
- **Flickr:** A direct link to Flickr for easy photo viewing.

- **Podcasting:** A tool that allows people to listen to audios as podcasts.
- **Related posts:** This shows posts that are related to the one you are reading.

Tas Tip

Visit www.marketinginthemomentbook.com to find more of the top plug-ins.

Checklist
Blogging:

Check off the steps as you go, so you make sure you've covered everything!

- ☐ Decide which type of blog platform you want to use: www.WordPress.com, www.Blogger.com, or www.TypePad.com.

- ☐ Hire a designer to make your blog match your brand.

- ☐ Trick out your blog with all the latest and greatest plug-ins.

- ☐ Add an RSS feed and a place for people to opt-in to your Web site.

- ☐ Start adding quality content to the blog in written, audio, and video form.

- ☐ Make sure your content is tagged with proper keywords (using the SEO plug-in).

- ☐ Submit each post to various social-bookmarking sites. www.SocialMarker.com is a great free tool to accomplish this task quickly.

☐ Monitor your analytics to see which posts are getting the most visits and comments, and put out more content around that topic. Give the people what they are looking for!

☐ E-mail your mailing list asking people to leave comments on your blog. This gets the community interaction flowing.

☐ Keep your blog updated often. Our recomendation is five to ten blog posts every week (including holidays).

Case Study

Randy wanted to become the top real-estate agent in Tampa, Florida. He set up a Web site and started doing some social marketing, SEO, and link building, but he was not getting much traction. His Web site was averaging only about 10 visits per day, or about 300 each month. We (Taz Solutions, Inc.) set him up a rocking WordPress blog with the focus of educating the marketplace rather than being in their face 24/7 and constantly selling. His Web site was focused on promoting his current listings and generating his new listings. But the blog also shared useful information, including the best places to eat in Tampa, the ratings of the various school districts, and the advantages of living in Tampa versus other places in the United States.

The Result: In three weeks, Randy's blog was averaging 175 unique visits per day. His listings increased by 25%, and his properties started selling faster than those of any other agents in his office.

The Takeaway: A blog combined with some great content can produce results very quickly. In many instances, traffic to your blog site will actually be greater than to your main Web site.

The Shift from Blogging to Microblogging

Although blogging continues to be one of the most effective marketing strategies that can be employed, it is critical to note that a shift is taking place. Instead of content writers focusing most of their time on formatting and crafting traditional, lengthy blog posts, they are supplementing that content with microblog posts. These posts can be made from anywhere in the world and are much shorter in length, typically under 200 characters.

Continue to use your blog as a marketing tactic, but offer up these condensed snippets in microblog format and you'll be capturing market share from your competition, because most are still not using microblogging.

Some of your target readers would prefer to read a 1,000-word article. Others just want the one or two key points in that article. With microblogging, you're capturing both kinds of audiences—and potential customers.

The great thing about microblogging is that it can be done from anywhere in the world. Simply send in a text message and your post is instantly live. This beats spending three hours trying to format the post in WordPress or Blogger on your tiny BlackBerry screen! Yes, you can blog from your phone as well, but it's much easier to send in a 200-character message versus a 500-word post. This allows you to capture your thoughts *in the moment* wherever you are!

Mass syndication has also greatly contributed to the rise of microblogging. Mass syndication means having your content go to multiple places with the push of one button. Many of the top social-networking Web sites allow you to update your status or input some key information that alerts your network of the update. These updates are always limited in character length. A blog article would be too lengthy. A 200-character post fits just perfectly. Essentially, what this allows is making one microblog post to then update 20 social-networking applications instantly!

Twitter and How It's Changing the World

There is a pretty good chance you have heard of Twitter, because it has been mentioned on *Good Morning America,* CNBC, and CNN, to name a few. It was talked about all through the most recent election, has been quoted in movies, and even has been referenced on a variety of the current hit TV shows. Terms such as *tweet* and *status update* are now common language. There is even a conference devoted 100% to Twitter called the 140 conference (www.140conf.com). According to their Web site, the original scope of #140conf was to explore "the effects of Twitter on: Celebrity, "The Media," Advertising, and (maybe) Politics." Over time, the scope expanded to look at the effects of Twitter on topics ranging from public safety to public diplomacy. What has really given Twitter the steam it needs to survive as a long-standing successful Web 3.0 company is the fact that it's totally different from everything we're used to. The norm has been search-engine-friendly articles, long blog content, and even longer press releases. The founders of Twitter (Evan Williams and Biz Stone) knew that people were lacking time and getting frustrated with the status quo, so they decided to shake things up a bit. The shake up: No more long content allowed. Anything you want to say must be 140 characters or fewer. The result: People have been flocking to Twitter like there's no tomorrow!

What Is Twitter?

"Twitter is a service for friends, family, and coworkers to communicate and stay connected through the exchange of quick, frequent answers to one simple question: What are you doing?"

That is the definition provided by www.Twitter.com, but it doesn't do it justice. Twitter has outgrown the vision of the people who originated it, and it has become a place to find long-lost friends, connect with your favorite authors, build raving fans, get instant feedback, launch new products, and build long-lasting relationships. You have both ends of the spectrum: social networking and microblogging. In other words, you can have the social connection with people, but you're able to do it with much smaller amounts of text. Obviously, the use of Twitter easily scales past the idea of updating people on "what you are doing."

On Twitter, there are three key terms you need to know: *followers*, *following*, and *tweets*. *Following* refers to the people you personally are tracking and want to be kept up-to-date on. *Followers* are those people who want to be kept in the know about what you're doing. Lastly, *tweets* are the updates broadcasted to your followers. These updates are strictly limited to 140 total characters. This makes it a microblog post.

Other Twitter lingo you need to be aware of:

- **Status:** Your update to "what are you currently doing?."
- **Direct Message:** Conversations that are private between you and another user.
- **@Tweets:** Public responses to others' tweets.
- **Retweets:** What you have when you take someone else's messages and broadcast them to your followers.
- **TinyURL:** A tool that shortens your long links automatically.
- **Tweeps** (for good measure): Your Twitter peeps.

Who Should Be Using Twitter?

Anyone who is looking to generate more sales or leads for their business should be using Twitter. Twitter has exploded to millions of users across the globe. Many of these users are your perfect target market! You do not need to own a company or be a businessperson to be on Twitter. In fact, Twitter was started for people to use it more on the social scene. They envisioned friends and family following one another to be able to easily see what the other is doing and to share thoughts. Entrepreneurs saw beyond this and started using it for marketing purposes. After entrepreneurs started making traction and spreading the word about Twitter's ease of use, others started flocking to the Web site. You will find speakers, authors, consultants, CEOs, companies, brands, students, teachers, professors, scientists, skydivers, and philanthropists on the site. The bottom line is that Twitter can be used by anyone and everyone.

How to Get a Massive Number of Twitter Followers

When you log in to Twitter, you are prompted to update your status by answering the question "What are you doing?."

I want you think of this totally differently. Instead of taking such a generalized approach, update your status with responses to the following:

- What are you currently interested in?
- What are you currently reading?
- What project(s) are you currently working on?
- In what contest are you participating?
- What new products are you releasing?
- What's new in your life?
- What's new with your family?
- Pose questions.

Update your status to position yourself as an engaging thought leader who wants to stimulate conversation and activity; for example:

> Currently reading *Think and Grow Rich*. A very insightful book, don't you think?

> Working on my new book on Web 3.0 marketing. I hope you'll purchase it when it's in stores.

The key concept in growing your Twitter followers is to give your followers tweets of value. This may sound basic, but if you don't grab this concept, all the other Twitter tactics I'm going to give you will be useless. Give your followers reasons to read your tweets and the rest will fall into place.

To Do

How to Get Started with Twitter:

Step 1: *Go to https://Twitter.com/ and sign up.*

Step 2: *Choose a username.*

We recommend using your first and last name—for example, michaeltasner. If this is an account for a business, use the business name—for example, tazsolutions.

Step 3: *Create your profile.*

This should be consistent across your various social-marketing sites for branding purposes. Because Twitter asks you to keep things short, make sure every word you use has been crafted perfectly. Tell people what you do and how you can support them or solve their problems. The most critical part of your profile is your Web site link. You get one link—make sure it's your main Web site or where you want to send the bulk of your traffic.

Tas Tip

When you come from a place of "How can I support you?" as opposed to "This is what I do," your prospects will be much more attracted to you, and your sales will go up.

Step 4: *Make your profile visually appealing.*

Have a design firm create a custom Twitter background using your photo, product, or logo. Include links under those photos. Twitter does not allow any type of hard links in your background image, so list your Web site address, Facebook profile, blog, and even LinkedIn or any of the other sites you use frequently. You can also take advantage of www.TwitterPatterns.com if you are looking for a free solution for the short term.

For some examples of great uses of the Twitter background opportunity, check out the following:

- www.twitter.com/michaeltasner
- www.twitter.com/matthew_ferry
- www.twitter.com/suzeormanshow

Step 5: *Sync your e-mail with Twitter to gain instant Twitter followers.*

This will alert people on your e-mail list that you have Twitter so that they can start following you.

Step 6: *Link your cellphone with Twitter.*

Simply click on Add a Device from the Twitter Web site when you're logged in, and follow the instructions from there. This will allow you to text message tweets from wherever you are, assuming you have an international cell phone.

Step 7: *Start tweeting.*

Once a day is the minimum. I encourage you to tweet six to eight times each day. Keep in mind that these are 140-character tweets. How long could it take to pop those out? Frequency is important because it allows you to build a following of loyal readers who get to view different types of material. It also gives you more potential viral material for others to talk about and spread for you.

Step 8: *Increase the number of people you are following.*

It is common Twitter practice for many of the people you are following to follow you in return. The quickest way to find some fun people to follow is to do a search on Twitter.

For example: Say you sell pet products. Do a quick search for PETCO to see who is following them. Begin following some of those people. Yes, this is very much like friend trolling, but it's a great way to start building your account quickly.

Step 9: *Integrate your blog with Twitter.*

This will allow your blog to update Twitter each time you post. This is a great way to send traffic back to your blog.

Step 10: *Step it up a notch.*

Leverage some (or all) of the advanced Twitter tactics shown next to continue rocking Twitter.

Advanced Twitter-Building Tactics and Other Twitter Tools

Here are some different advanced tactics and tools to help build out your Twitter presence.

@Tweets

@Tweets are messages that show up in a fellow Twitter user's account, but are public and not direct messages. These typically are simple replies to something someone else has said. Sending these shows that you want to be a part of the Twitter tribe, and you are taking time to read people's tweets.

Direct Messages

Direct Messages are the equivalent of e-mail, but they must maintain the same character restriction. We like to send out 50 direct messages a day to our random Twitter followers with something of value. These direct messages are very similar to our tweets. The only difference is that they are customized slightly to the person to whom we are sending them.

Retweeting

Retweeting is simply taking someone else's tweet and rebroadcasting it to your followers. I use retweeting in two ways. The first way is by giving credit or props to others who are supplying good information. An example of what this would look like is as follows:

Retweet: @tonyrobbins The way to success http://www. linktohisposthere.com—great advice

The second way I use retweets is to ask people to retweet a link for me. It may be a blog post I recently published or a new product or service. This tactic not only helps increase my Twitter following, but also helps me get hundreds of links pointing to my material.

Tweet Deck

Tweet Deck is your personal browser for staying in touch with what's happening now. It connects you and your contacts on Twitter, as well as on Facebook, allowing you to see everything in one place. I like to use this to scan for topics of interest, a process similar to using search.twitter.com (explained shortly). The key difference is that I'm seeing only people with whom I'm connected. Rather, with search.twitter.com, you are seeing the entire Twitter universe. It's a very handy tool, but I warn you, it can be addicting. When you start getting thousands of followers, Tweet Deck will be constantly getting updated; it becomes very challenging to stay on top of all your followers' tweets.

I recommend using Tweet Deck once or twice each day. Scan some of the most recent posts and send some direct messages and @Tweets, and pop out a few tweets of your own.

Social Oomph

Social Oomph (formerly Tweet Later) allows you to automatically send a welcome or thank-you message to people who follow you and automatically follows them as opposed to your having to do it manually.

Here are the instructions boiled down for you:

1. Go to www.socialoomph.com.
2. Sign up for an account.
3. After signing up, log in to your Social Oomph account.
4. Click on Manage My Scheduled Tweets and Twitter Account Automation.
5. Click on Add Account.
6. Select/type Twitter and click Next.
7. Enter your Twitter username and password.

8. Click on Auto Welcome and enter a welcome message in the box.

9. Check the option for auto-follow and auto-unfollow.

10. Click on Save and you have successfully set up Social Oomph.

Search.twitter.com

Search.twitter.com is one of my favorite tools out there to build highly targeted followers. It allows you to type in various words and phrases and see all the people who are tweeting about that word/phrase or topic. Why is this capability valuable? It lets you find out what's currently hot!

Here are some examples of phrases:

Search Phrase	Who Might Be Interested
Looking for a home	Real-estate agent
Life insurance	Insurance agent
New shoes	www.Zappos.com
The election	President Barack Obama
Child safety	Fisher-Price

Think about the different phrases your prospects or customers would be searching for and take action:

- **Action #1:** Start following others. Hopefully they will follow you in return.

- **Action #2:** Send an @Tweet showing them you also want to join in on the conversation.

Here is a recent example of how we landed a new marketing client:

Search Phrase: *Work from home.*

Ten minutes later, we had a direct message, and two hours later we were on the phone with Steve, coaching him about his new business from home selling high-end stuffed animals.

Twitturly

Twitturly tracks the top URLs that are being talked about on Twitter. This has come in handy to find out what is being said about our company and our competitors, and even to find some of the latest trends on the Web.

Multiple Twitter Accounts

Having multiple Twitter accounts is highly recommended, especially if you have different client bases and play in multiple markets. I personally have six Twitter accounts: a personal account for close friends/family, two for Taz Solutions, Inc., one for this book, one for corporate clients, and one where I simply follow other Internet-marketing experts. With multiple accounts comes more work, but between these accounts I have more than 100,000 followers! I can go even deeper to say that these are 100,000 targeted Twitter followers, because I was very selective as to whom I would follow and allow to follow me for each of the accounts.

Twitter Maintenance

As with every social network, there is some daily maintenance involved. With Twitter, because the tweets are so short, the maintenance is relatively minimal. Here are the daily tasks you want to make sure you are on top of:

Check and respond to all direct messages. These messages will be in a section called Direct Messages (go figure). Simply click on the link and you will see all of your direct messages. Keep in mind that many of these will be cookie-cutter replies from people you started following. As mentioned, we recommend you do the same thing using Social Oomph, but the difference is that your direct messages will be much more impactful than most of the ones you will receive. Be careful when checking over your messages. In other words, don't get "delete happy."

After your Twitter following starts to evolve rapidly, you will receive direct messages asking sales-related questions and very likely will close some business solely from Twitter. Treat these direct messages as if they were e-mail. Because the 140-character limit can get annoying, we like to ask for an e-mail address so that we can provide a more lengthy reply. This also further qualifies the lead/prospect.

Delete direct messages after you have read them.

Check and respond to any @Tweets. The worst thing you can do is not respond to a direct message or a direct tweet. Keep the conversations going and let others know you care and enjoyed their message.

Keep your followers and following clean. When you start using advanced tools like Social Oomph, you are going to have some weird, spam-related, and somewhat questionable people following you. To remove people you don't want following you, simply click on Followers when logged in to your account, locate the user, and then click Block. To stop following people, click on Following and Remove next to the user you no longer want to follow.

Remove people who are not following you. It's good Twitter practice for someone you are following to follow you, too. If after 48 business hours they have decided to not follow you back, simply remove them. This is done to ensure you do not exceed the maximum number of people you can have following you in proportion to the people you are following.

Tweet often. No lecture needed here. If you tweet and provide tweets of value, this tactic will become like second nature.

Here are seven other simple ways to build your Twitter presence:

- Add your Twitter address to your e-mail signature file.
- Promote your address across your other social-marketing sites.
- Send an e-mail blast to your mailing list asking them to follow you and to tell their friends about the great content that's available on your Twitter site.
- Organize a contest through your Twitter account. If followers refer others to follow you, they get a contest entry.
- Send a press release through www.PRWeb.com announcing your Twitter presence.
- Pitch people with very large Twitter followings, asking them to send a short tweet about you and offering to do the same in return.
- Get on the news and mention your Twitter address.

The content shift is here. Don't stop blogging or releasing articles. But add microblogging to your many avenues for getting your message out. Twitter is quickly becoming one of the top social networks in the world.

 ## Case Study

Dwan Bent-Twyford is a real-estate-education teacher, author, and mentor. She and her husband, Bill, are among the top trainers in the world on short sales, fore-closures, and real estate investing. Dwan and Bill's second book, *How to Sell a House When It's Worth Less Than the Mortgage*, was recently released. Typically with the release of a book, it's a great idea to do a major book-launch campaign. They had a nice size e-mail list, and also had some people onboard to help, but their secret weapon was Twitter. Between their two Twitter accounts, they reached more than 15,000 people. Because this was a time-sensitive deal, we hammered out more than 50 updates on Twitter promoting the launch in just a few days.

The Result: Hundreds of sales came from their loyal Twitter following. The best part: Their book occupied the top three spots in the investments category on www.Amazon.com!

The Takeaway: Twitter can be leveraged in various ways, especially if you have a loyal following and give your Tweeps a reason to watch you.

4

Mobile Marketing: Tapping into Billions of Cellphone Users

Mobile marketing is among my favorite Web 3.0 marketing tactics, because it is expanding at the fastest rate and also has the most upside potential. The icing on the cake: Fewer than 6% of businesses are doing any type of mobile marketing. If you look at companies doing less than $10 million per year, that percentage drops even more drastically to nearly .05%. What does this mean to you? Now is the best time to start leveraging mobile marketing, because it's still relatively new in the eyes of both marketers and consumers.

What Is Mobile Marketing?

When I refer to mobile marketing in this book, I'm referring to marketing on a mobile device, such as receiving a text message from a vendor with a promotional code, buying products right from your BlackBerry, or viewing picture messages that depict a product you may be interested in. There is also a second, more traditional definition of mobile marketing that describes marketing in a moving fashion. An example of this would be moving billboards. Travel to any major city and you will see many examples of both types of mobile marketing. Just note that, in going forward, we're solely talking about mobile devices. Okay, good. We have that cleared up.

There are various marketing methods with mobile phones, the most popular being SMS, or short messaging service (text messages). Other forms of mobile marketing include MMS (multimedia messaging service), in-game marketing, and mobile Web marketing.

Mobile Marketing with SMS

Let's start with the most popular method: SMS.

Marketing on a mobile phone has become much more popular since the rise of SMS, or short message service. This rise began in the early 2000s in Europe and parts of Asia when businesses started to gather mobile phone numbers of consumers. With these mobile numbers in hand, they started blasting out content (whether people requested the content or not). What they found was that this really was a channel with some major legs to grow and expand. Surprisingly, consumers were actually happy to receive text messages from businesses they had visited. This eliminated the whole permission marketing constraint because very few people objected. In fact, many who didn't receive the text messages felt left out and wanted to join the list!

In the past few years, SMS marketing has become a much more accepted advertising channel, but one that few businesses use. One of the many reasons SMS, or mobile marketing in general, has started to become accepted into society is that it's policed much more than e-mail. The carriers (Verizon, AT&T, Sprint, and so on), who watch over their networks, have set guidelines and precedents for the mobile-marketing industry. Open your e-mail inbox and look at how many spam messages you have. In the past 24 hours,

I have received 552 spam e-mails. Take a look at your mobile device; how many spam messages do you have in your text messaging inbox? I have zero.

As SMS marketing continued to grow, the mobile community wanted to come up with another way to simplify the communication. Over the past few years, mobile short codes have been increasingly popular as a new channel to communicate with the mobile consumer. Businesses have started to treat the mobile short code as a type of mobile domain name allowing consumers to text a message at an event, in the store, or right off their packaging. For example, Verizon Wireless tends to run different promotions allowing customers to send a text message to receive a percentage off their next purchase. They have various signs in their stores, so while you're waiting, why not grab a mobile coupon code?

SMS services normally run off a short code, but sending text messages to an e-mail address is another tactic. These codes are five- or six-digit numbers that have been assigned by all the mobile operators in a given country for the use of brand campaigns and other consumer services.

So the gist of mobile marketing through SMS is two-fold:

1. When given permission, you can capture mobile numbers and send SMS advertisements, special offers, and information to consumers.

2. Short codes can be used for various types of promotions.

Mobile Marketing with MMS

MMS stands for multimedia messaging service, a telecommunications standard for sending messages that include multimedia objects such as images, audio, video, and rich text. When I think of MMS, I think of picture messaging.

When it comes down to it, MMS is simply an extension of SMS. All phones that have a color screen have the capability to send and receive MMS messages.

There are various cool marketing uses for MMS. One example is at the House of Blues. The brand allows visitors to send their mobile photos to the LED board, located live, and then House of Blues staffers blog about the various images online.

MMS marketing can help in all areas, from increasing brand recognition to more sales, deeper interactivity, and increasing event attendance.

I recently sent out a short 20-second MMS to my list of 24,000 mobile numbers asking them to comment on my tweet. The result: 4,252 responses and more than 25,000 retweets! Another example was The Investors Edge University sending an MMS message to remind people to attend their webinar. The result: 60% more people attended live than ever before!

In-Game Mobile Marketing

Mobile users are starting to play video games across their phones in real time with other users. This is similar to people being able to play games against each other using a video game system like PlayStation or Xbox. Gamers are finding an increasing number of sponsored ads across some of these games produced for mobile devices. If your target audience might be playing games, find the various games they frequent and contact the advertising department to see what the different rates are. In a perfect world, you will pay only for clicks on your ad rather than a flat rate.

Mobile Web Marketing

The standard term *mobile Web marketing*, in this instance, refers to placing ads on the mobile Web, very similar to the ads you see when browsing Google or Yahoo!. The Mobile Marketing Association does provide a set of guidelines and standards giving the recommended format of ads, presentation, and metrics used in reporting. Google, Yahoo!, and other content providers that have been selling advertising placement for years are now shifting to mobile-ad placement, and it's really starting to catch on.

Mobile Marketing Guidelines

One of the biggest advantages to mobile marketing is not only that the carriers are keeping an eye on the whole industry, but that the Mobile Marketing Association is quite active as well. The association is committed to helping advertisers make more money using mobile marketing while helping protect consumers from being spammed.

These are the key guidelines of mobile marketing (according to the MMA):

- Consumers need to be a double opt-in and have the ability to opt out at any time (similar to e-mail). Only they can decide whether they want to receive your information.

- Respecting consumer privacy should be your number-one concern. If this gets out of hand, mobile marketing will go right out the window.

- The information collected needs to be handled with the utmost concern to security and privacy and must be up to par with the laws of that location on handling customer data.

- If there is a contest or something of that nature, it should be explained so that consumers know if there are fees or other commitments on their part (certain language must be used).

- Marketing to anyone under the age of 13 brings up many ethical questions and is a major issue.

Marketers, who like to dance on the wild side, prefer limited regulation. In fact, the can-spam laws put tens of thousands of marketers out of business overnight and many in jail. With stricter regulation, consumers can get information they actually want or request, thus helping open rates, adoption rates, and sales. The few legitimate marketers in the industry who take the regulations and guidelines to heart are the ones here to stay. The fly-by-night companies will continue to bite the dust.

A World Run on BlackBerrys, iPhones, and Mobile Devices

Take a look around when you're on the subway, at a conference, at a party, or even at a concert. Chances are, without trying, you'll spot various mobile devices.

There are more than four billion, yes that's *billion*, cellphone users in the world, as reported by the United Nations International Telecommunications Union. There are roughly six billion people on the planet. So doing the math, over 60% of people in the world have some type of mobile device. Mobile is huge.

Just think of the possibilities. Consumers are relying more and more on their mobile devices as their devices continue to get smarter and smarter. The other thing you should keep in mind is that that number is factoring in all the impoverished places in the world. When you look at countries like the United States, Spain, the United Kingdom, and so on, the percentage of users in ratio to the population in those locations is upwards of 90% and, in many countries, at or above 100%. This means there are more cellphones in use than people using them!

There are two devices that have received the most media attention, and they deserve the attention for a reason. They have changed the way we do business and have opened many doors of new possibilities. The first device is the BlackBerry, produced by a company called Research in Motion (RIM), and the second is the iPhone, by Apple.

BlackBerrys

Specifically, BlackBerry is a collection of wireless, hand-held devices that was brought to market in 1999. It was first introduced solely as a two-way pager. Just three years later, BlackBerry released its first smartphone with the ability to get e-mail, surf the Web, send faxes, and send and receive text (SMS) and picture messages (MMS). The original intention was to target executives and focus on one of its core functionalities: the capability to have e-mail anywhere you want on the go, assuming that a wireless network is in the vicinity. In reality, it was for the corporate market because the prices were so high that individuals were not really purchasing the devices.

Currently, there are 32 million BlackBerry users. This is up from 12 million in 2007. There are various reasons for the upward shift, with the most prevalent being the ability to take life with you (one of BlackBerry's tag lines). The price point of BlackBerrys has also come down considerably, making them more widely accepted by consumers as opposed to strictly businesspeople. This device can do it all.

When I travel, I do take a laptop with me. But more often than not, I rely on my BlackBerry to get me through the day. I can receive urgent e-mails, browse the Web, grab my faxes, check Facebook, and even get instant messages right from a phone that fits neatly in my pocket. Need to verify meetings? No problem! My Google calendar pushes right to my BlackBerry and updates in real time, in case my assistant makes some changes.

How much more powerful of a device can you get? The device is so powerful; users typically get "addicted" to using their BlackBerrys too often and have coined the term "CrackBerry." This is the notion that you are now connected 100% of the time, 24/7. Some of you think this is a good thing, and others will disagree. I'll let you be the judge of that!

BlackBerry Apps

You will continue to learn about apps (short for applications) throughout this book, but I want to briefly touch on BlackBerry apps. In trying to keep up with the iPhone, BlackBerry has been rocking out Blackberry apps. Developers and companies can design apps for the BlackBerry, allowing its users to have the software at their fingertips. The intention with using apps is to continue to make your BlackBerry a more and more powerful device and truly an all-in-one solution.

Some of my favorite applications for the BlackBerry include these:

- **Facebook:** I can update my status, upload photos, and post on my friends' walls from wherever I am.
- **Salesforce.com:** It's great to see critical customer information without my laptop.
- **Hotel organizer:** This enables me to search through thousands of hotels, checking availability and rates. I've been stranded a few times, and this has saved me.

The number of applications is going to continue to rise as time goes on. Before you know it, there will be applications that allow you to check your dry cleaning status, turn on your hot tub with the push of a button, get an updated financial report, trade stocks without having to be logged in to your broker account, host meetings where others can see your BlackBerry screen, and so on. The possibilities are endless!

Case Study

Tim runs an online magazine that focuses on teaching people how to live and invest overseas. As you might assume, he travels all the time. He will recommend only places he or someone on his staff has personally visited and learned about in great detail. The problem is that many of these places are highly remote. His magazine claims to have information on some of the most secluded places in the world. Rather than missing a week or two of critical e-mails and updates on the happenings around the office while on the road, he runs his company with his BlackBerry! The Internet connection is not nearly as quick as it is at home, but heck, what's the rush? He also has various apps installed on his Blackberry that allow him to communicate with his clients and prospects. Whether he's tweeting about his journey or using the camera to stream a video via Ustream.TV, he doesn't miss any potential marketing opportunities while abroad.

Key Points:

- You can take your life with you, anywhere you go in the world, without missing a beat.

- A smartphone, like the BlackBerry, provides wireless access to pretty much anything you need.

- A pocket-size phone is much easier to carry than a bulky laptop.

- There are various applications that can be utilized for marketing purposes.

iPhones

I started off talking about BlackBerrys for two reasons:
(1) I own one, and (2) I saved the best for last.

Yes, I'll admit it openly right now: I bow down to the iPhone.
I do love my BlackBerry, but I'm counting down the days
until I will be able to purchase an iPhone without having to
switch from the superior service provider (in my opinion),
Verizon.

The iPhone is manufactured and sold by Apple. What has
really driven demand for the iPhone is the fact that the
device is essentially a smartphone and iPod in one.

Before I get into too many more details about the iPhone,
here are the key differences in comparing this device to the
BlackBerry:

- No keypad. Instead, it has a touchscreen.
- iPod technology with built-in 8GB, 16GB, or 32GB of
  storage.
- 75,000-plus applications available.

In comparing the two devices, both have their advantages
and disadvantages. And it's really a choice based on user
preference. Because the BlackBerry has been around for a
while, it does have the technology down pretty cold. It has
also mastered e-mail. Apple, on the other hand, really
wanted to involve developers to make the iPhone more of an
open-source platform and play out the iPod's "sex appeal"
and popularity factor. The choice is yours. If I had my way,
I'd own both, with one on each hip!

The iPhone is picking up speed in terms of sales and applications that have been built on its platform. To date, more
than 32 million units have been sold. Compare that to the
number of BlackBerry users, and, to me, it looks like we've
got a pretty even race on our hands as to which device will
become the smartphone of choice.

The limiting factor of iPhone sales has been the fact that they can be used only on a certain network, AT&T (Cingular at its introduction). It is possible to unlock the iPhone to make it available for use with other carriers. It's been noted that 25% of iPhones sold have not been registered with AT&T. I don't recommend doing this (you void your warranty), but if you really want to use an iPhone with a different carrier, it can be done.

What's shocking is the number of sales compared to the amount of time the iPhone has actually been available. The iPhone has been on the market only since January 2007, when Steve Jobs first released the device. Since then, the device has gone through a few revisions to its current 3GS model, which is available with 8GB, 16GB, and 32GB of storage. And the iPod Touch has joined the product line as basically an iPhone without the phone or camera—but with access to the apps.

iPhone Apps

Besides being a multimedia device, phone, and iPod all in one, the biggest selling point of the iPhone is the huge number of applications available for your iPhone (or iPod Touch). Some of the applications are free and others are one-time or low-cost monthly fees.

Apple says, "You will love your iPhone because it's a phone, an iPod, and an Internet device in one. It gives you access to thousands of applications. And it's built on technology that's years ahead of its time." That claim is 100% accurate and has been the driving force of the company. They have applications that will help in all facets of your life:

- Around your house:
  - **Home Sizer:** Calculates the area of your room to aid in decorating before you go to the store.
  - **eBay:** Stay up to speed on all your eBay auctions.

- **Cooking:** Find all the recipes you need at your fingertips.
- For working out:
  - **iMapMyRide:** Records every mile you ride on your bike.
  - **Yoga Stretch:** A yoga instructor who travels with you.
  - **iPump Pilates:** Strengthen and tone your abs with a Pilates instructor.
- For managing money:
  - **Bloomberg:** Need to check your stocks? Now you can.
  - **www.Mint.com app:** One of the best free places to manage money.
  - **Bank Locator:** Need to know where the nearest bank is? Now you can in seconds!
- For going out:
  - **GPark:** Ever forget where you parked? Never again, if you have this app!
  - **YP Mobile:** This allows you to find concerts, events, and other happenings.
  - **Shazam:** Trying to think of the name of a song? Hold your iPhone up to the radio (or even at a concert), and it will tell you what song is playing!
- For traveling:
  - **TravelTracker:** Put your entire trip itinerary in so you can relax, knowing that the details are covered.
  - **Currency:** Convert any currency instantly.
  - **SodaSnap:** Turn your photos into digital post-cards.

- For getting things done:
  - **OmniFocus (this is my favorite):** This power application will detect where you are currently located, and compile lists related to your tasks based on your location. Say, for example, on your task list is *visit the bank and the grocery store.* This app will create the lists in order based on your current location!
  - **Air Sharing:** Share any documents and drag and drop to a computer instantly.
  - **1Password:** Store all your passwords in one place.
- For fun and games:
  - **Texas Hold 'Em:** Win some money playing poker!
  - **YouTube:** Check out some crazy videos.
  - **Scrabble:** Play one of America's favorite games.

One key point to keep in mind is that many applications are developed by companies solely for capturing the prospect information. They then leverage this information to try to sell you some of their other products and services.

The reason I went through these different applications was to show you some of the thousands available. The iPhone is one of the most powerful devices ever created. Reread those applications to see what you can do with it. If you look a few years into the future (which is my specialty), the iPhone is positioning itself to be the one device you need to carry—nothing more, nothing less. It is the one device that will store your entire life and have applications to accomplish the job. It is everything you need to do. I love my BlackBerry, but they have a lot of catching up to do!

Five years ago, it wasn't a big deal if your Web site was not mobile compliant. Today, it's a necessity. As more and more people continue to purchase smartphones, you need to make sure your Web site is ready for their visits. If you have browsed a Web site from a mobile device, you will understand that it is a completely different ballgame. Images often don't show up, Flash can be disastrous, and text becomes hard to read. You need to keep in mind that you're browsing the Web on a four-inch screen rather than a computer monitor—even the smallest monitors display Web sites more clearly than smartphones.

Because you are going to be on the leading edge in marketing, this is an essential step in Web 3.0 marketing. Since this is a marketing and strategy book, rather than a programming book, I will not provide all the crazy codes to install on your Web site. Instead, I'll give you the steps that need to be accomplished and then ask you to hire a designer and programmer to make them happen. The good thing is that this is not overly expensive by any means!

The first thing you need to decide is whether you want to modify the code on your existing Web site, or use a totally new Web site, designed specifically for mobile devices. Since we are going to make your competition nonexistent (and quite frankly irrelevant), you are going to go with option two. The reasoning behind this is that modifying your existing code is fine, but having a separate site devoted solely to mobile will give you a better edge against the competition and show the marketplace you're serious about mobile marketing.

Designing a Web site specifically for mobile devices—this is the route to take to ensure optimum success.

 ## To Do

Establishing a Mobile-Only Site:

Step 1: *Establish a domain name.*

Go to www.GoDaddy.com (or any other domain-name registration service) and grab yourdomainname.mobi. Mobile is signified by the .mobi.

Step 2: *Plan your content.*

Make a mind map showing the content you want on this new Web site. There are various things to keep in mind when doing so:

- Decide what information is essential to convey (location, contact information, product information).

- This site should be a much more boiled-down version of your current Web site. The areas that typically get omitted are presentations heavy in Flash, video intros or walk-ons, unique or funky Web coding that is not the norm, and pages that are not critical. For example, having photos and bios of the executive staff might not be a critical page to be added to your mobile page.

- You still want people to be able to purchase your products right from their device.

- Know which of your target markets will be using this mobile site and cater it a bit more to them.

- In terms of the design elements, when deciding on content and information, you also need to keep these factors in mind:

  - Keep videos and flash off this site.

  - Get rid of any type of animations.

  - Keep images to a minimum.

  - Make sure that the site is heavy on the text and you pay particular attention to formatting and sizing.

You want to make sure that the content is enough to convey your message, gives visitors the critical information they need, and allows customers to purchase your products. Don't make your mobile site too minimal! Keep up your branding and your image, but keep it simple.

Step 3: *Ask a professional.*

Take your finalized mind map and hand it off to a qualified design and programming firm that also fully understands marketing. They will most likely be coding the site using a language called XML/XHTML and CSS. There are different ways to code a mobile site, but simplicity is the most important thing to keep in mind. The designers should also understand that this should open well in all the different browsers that smartphones sport. Your Web site should look perfect across a wireless PDA, a BlackBerry, an iPhone, or any other device that offers access to the Internet.

Step 4: *Let your visitors know you've gone mobile.*

Put a link on your existing Web site that says, "Browsing from a mobile device? Click here." That link will then take them to your new mobile site.

Step 5: *Advertise!*

Advertise your .mobi link in your branding messages as well. Not only do you have a .com, but you also sport a fancy .mobi!

How to Implement Mobile Marketing

Unlike many of the other tactics discussed in this book, mobile marketing has quite a few different angles. Some will apply to your business, others will not. But with mobile, pick a few, follow the how-to instructions, and implement.

SMS

SMS, or a text message, is one of the easiest ways to start gaining traction in the mobile marketing world. Text messages have a 95% to 100% open rate! In contrast, with e-mail marketing, the highest open rate I have ever seen is 74%. But, sadly, the average open rate of an e-mail is around 10%.

The other great thing about SMS marketing is that the messages are short, so they are typically read in full. You'd be smart to have a very specific, focused message in your text.

Keeping People Up-to-Date

Most businesses have some type of e-newsletter. But they may not be using their newsletter to its fullest advantage. My guess is that only 1 out of 10,000-plus businesses collect mobile numbers on their Web site opt in, product/service literature, or in their stores. Start collecting mobile numbers so you can send a short, every-now-and-then message about the happenings of your business and upcoming events.

Here's an example of a good message: Taz Solutions, Inc., is now offering 10% off Web site packages. Visit www.tazsol.com to find out more or call 1-800-659-3020.

Special Offers

Need to announce a special product offering, a short promotion, or a discount code? With a very high open rate (and a short delay in opening), popping out specials to your mobile list through a text message will stir up some action!

Hold a Contest

"Submit your mobile number and be entered into a contest to win *(fill in a fantastic prize here)."* It's a great way to capture numbers in a nonthreatening way. (Just make sure you have all your legal ducks in a row. Hosting a contest can get legally complicated, but it can bring in some great results.)

Case Study

Instead of plugging in a case study here of how other companies have used text-messaging contests in their businesses, I want to include you in a contest we're having! When you bought this book, you automatically (with or without your knowing) got in line, if you will, for a free giveaway.

Go to www.marketinginthemomentbook.com to register. On this page, enter your mobile number, name, and e-mail. A text will be sent to your phone that tells you if you're the winner. Winner of what, you may be asking? We are giving away three high-end coaching/consulting packages absolutely free as a way of saying thank you for buying this book and participating in our contest!

Reminders

Text a short reminder for an upcoming event, promotion, or special you're offering—really anything for which you want to give your clients a friendly nudge/reminder.

Customer Service/Client Care

Wouldn't you love to get a text message from a recent appointment or sale saying, "Thank you so much for your business. We can't wait to be able to serve you again soon!"? I know I sure would. And to date, I have yet to receive a message like this.

Interaction

The key to social marketing is the interaction and making people feel welcome and part of something. As opposed to always being one-way with your SMS marketing, try out some interaction. Allow people to send text messages with various requests, ideas, thoughts, questions, and comments. Take it a step further and allow people to vote on particular topics! I saved this one for last, because I feel it has the biggest impact. When you involve your prospects and customers, they grow to further know, like, and trust you and your business. Visit marketinginthemomentbook.mobi to give me feedback on the book and to join the Web 3.0 Marketing community!

Case Study

txtCode Feedback is a product of SMS Feedback, an Australian company. Currently available only in the land down under, this is truly a revolutionary customer-feedback service that enables companies to collect feedback from consumers via text messaging. Consumers' text messages are converted into e-mail and sent to the desired e-mail recipient.

These are some of the benefits txtCode has generated for users:

- Capturing more customer feedback compared to traditional methods.

- Being able to easily categorize and review customer feedback as it's submitted.

- Being able to effectively identify the positive and negative outcomes of marketing campaigns.

- Creating improved customer satisfaction by exposing and eliminating negative aspects of the company.

- Empowering customers, thereby making them loyal.

- Increasing consumer and market perception by responding to customer feedback immediately.

To Do

How to Get Started with Mobile Marketing:

Step 1: *Find a text-messaging company.*

Sign up for a service that will allow you to capture and send and receive text messages in large quantities. Here are a few companies you can check out:

www.trumpia.com
www.mobilestorm.com
www.boomtext.com
www.mozeo.com

Some of these companies have one-time setup fees; for others, you can buy the license or even pay monthly fees based on your usage. Each of the companies has different product offerings. www.Trumpia.com, for example, has numerous additional offerings other than just mobile marketing. Check them out and search Google for other companies that offer similar services.

Step 2: *Get mobile numbers!*

Remember the statistics on how many people are carrying mobile phones? Chances are, 85% of people in your country will be carrying a mobile phone.

Start capturing mobile numbers instead of (or in addition to) land-line phone numbers. Here are eight ways to capture mobile numbers:

1. Ask for mobile numbers *everywhere*.

2. Let your customers and prospects know that they are part of an elite group who will be updated before anyone else (as long as this is true).

3. Offer a free gift in exchange for their number.

4. Ask people to refer a friend, providing their information as well, in exchange for a bonus or two.

5. Host a contest; to enter, contestants simply submit their name and mobile number.

6. Get them involved, allowing them to interact with you via text.

7. Pay them cash.

8. Reassure them that you won't be spamming them and that their information is kept secure, and watch your capture rates climb drastically.

Step 3: *Decide which marketing tactics you are going to employ.*

We use a combination of them all. Please keep in mind that we are always staying mobile compliant.

Step 4: *Keep your lists segmented if possible.*

Maintaining several different mobile phone lists allows you to further craft your messages to the exact target audience. Knowing who is using a smartphone versus who is not is also very powerful information. This allows you to craft messages with links for smartphone users and solely text messages for those who won't be able to view the link from their device.

Step 5: *Construct your message carefully and effectively.*

Because you're limited on the numbers of characters you can use, you need to make certain that your language is effective, direct, and to the point, causing users to take your desired action.

For example: *1-Day-Only Sale on All Jeans. 25% off when you mention the phrase "Blue Jeans." Expires at 10 PM.*

- Play with your verbiage several times. Before I send any message via text, I do at least 7 rewrites. When doing a massive promotion, I've done as many as 40. Every word needs to be crafted for maximum impact.

- Use Web site links selectively in case your prospects cannot view them on their particular phone. Use a service like www.TinyURL.com to make your links shorter, if they are long, to save on characters.

- Make sure you are providing information that is requested or that is of value, keeping in mind that many people still pay per text message.

Step 6: *Send the message.*

Step 7: *Repeat.*

Be careful with how many messages you send each month. We have tried as many as two messages a week and have had issues with negative response to the frequency. We now send two to four messages each month.

MMS

SMS messages are great, but MMS takes things up another notch with color, sound, and all sorts of interesting action.

Sending media-rich content is still a bit ahead of its time. But I still want to make sure you're on top of this. The reason it is just slightly futuristic is that many of the mobile phones are not set up to receive MMS messages and, in a way, that makes sense. The size of the files becomes an issue along with load time. Smartphones and newer cellphones have no issues loading most of the MMS content with ease. The most common types of MMS are images. Videos, rich text, and animation are also increasing in popularity.

There are six ways to integrate MMS marketing into your current tactics, which I'll cover next.

Special Offers/Discounts/Promotions

Special offers and discounts always seem to fare well in the mobile-marketing arena. Send a photo of an image that gives a special offer. To receive the offer, the recipient must either.

- Take action on the photo (visit a Web site, call a number)

  or

- Bring their phone to the store and show the actual coupon to receive the discount or special offer.

Case Study

BMW has always prided itself on staying on the leading edge of innovation. They also pride themselves on being masters at marketing. So much so, in fact, that they have vowed to test and use all the different mobile-marketing tactics. In 2008, they wanted to push their newly released snow tires. To test the waters, they sent an MMS message to different lists showing what the car they owned (down to the specific model) would look like with the new snow tires. Customers could also download an application to see how the tires would look on various other cars.

The Result: They achieved a 30% conversion rate and rated this campaign as one of their most successful ever!

Video Clips/Animated Clips

I'm sure you have seen video clips floating around. Typically they are funny jokes or risqué clips. There are so many things you can do with video. Check these out:

- A thank-you-for-your-business video
- New-product announcement

- New-store opening
- Limited-time special
- Birthday video
- Super-client testimonial

The sky is the limit when it comes to video. Keep the videos short, inoffensive, amusing, content-rich, and worthwhile. Don't simply send videos for the sake of sending videos.

Interaction

As with SMS, you can get some fun interaction going with MMS. Allow people to send in videos they took with their phones. Turn a simple campaign into a contest and give away some cool prizes. Invite customers to give video testimonials about what it's like working with you or using your products. Have people send in video questions to be posted on your site, and answer them live. Keeping the interaction flowing will keep the dollars coming in!

Audio Clips

We love video, but we also really love audio, because we're able to multitask while listening. It's much more challenging to multitask while watching a video. The audio clips can be informational, talking about specials, saying thank you, sending a birthday or holiday greeting, telling people where you are (a cool trip or great conference), and so on. It can be pretty much about anything you want.

How-To Information

Wouldn't it be great to get a short video or audio on how to use what you just purchased? This goes across all the different markets, from consumer goods to electronics to consumables and so much more. You walk into the store and pick up four high-end steaks, and two minutes later, you get an

MMS message with instructions on the best way to prepare your dinner, and even suggested sides or wine. How-to information is very well received in the marketplace. It makes for better customer relations as well as a solid opportunity for potential additional purchases.

Freebies

Who doesn't love a good freebie? You can send free applications, pictures, videos, audios—anything of value.

To Do

How to Get Started Sending MMS Messages:

Step 1: *Leverage MMS.*

The solution you are leveraging for SMS marketing should also have the capability to send MMS messages. If not, here are a few companies that specialize in sending MMS messages:

- www.trumpia.com
- www.InteractMobile.com
- www.Velti.com
- www.BluefishMobile.com

Step 2: *Tailor your content and approach.*

Look at your objective to decide which type of content to send and which approach to take. Whether the objective is branding, selling something, reminding consumers of an event or a promotion, or just providing information, the medium needs to be tailored.

Step 3: *Send the multimedia content.*

We have had the best success with the following:

- **Videos:** Under 30 seconds; keep them fun and engaging.

- **Audios:** Under 60 seconds; fun, engaging, informational.

- **Images:** For special offers that are time sensitive.

Step 4: *Repeat.*

I recommend you send one SMS or MMS message weekly to stay in touch.

Mobile Ads

The last area of mobile marketing is mobile ads. These ads are the same thing as the traditional ads you see on Google, Facebook, YouTube, and other sites. According to *eMarketer*, there are currently 405 million mobile-Internet users, and that number is expected to double within the next four years. So you have a ready, willing, and able audience—you just need to reach them. As more businesspeople and everyday consumers start to get the Internet on their phones, mobile ads (similar to traditional ads) will continue to grow.

As a business, you pay for certain keyword phrases when people click on your ad (called pay-per-click). Right now the ad spending across mobile devices is low. It's stated that in the next five years, mobile ads will account for about 5% to 10% of the global ad spending. This is a ripe opportunity for you. Because fewer people are advertising on mobile devices, you can get some really great keyword phrases for a fraction of the traditional cost.

To Do

How to Start Generating Revenue with Mobile Ads:

Step 1: *If you do not already have an account on Google AdWords, go to www.adwords.google.com and set one up.*

Google still maintains the vast majority of the market share. But here are four other popular places that accept mobile ads:

- Yahoo!

- Facebook

- YouTube

- MySpace

Step 2: *When creating the campaign on the particular advertiser, make sure you select Create a Mobile Ad.*

There is a different set of options on the advertiser sites that are strictly devoted to mobile.

Step 3: *Select the keywords you are going to target.*

In this case, less is more, but you need enough to test. Here are some free keyword-selector tools:

- www.GoodKeywords.com

- www.Wordtracker.com

- www.adwords.google.com/select/ KeywordToolExternal

Step 4: *Craft the ad, keeping in mind several guidelines:*

- Mobile text ads contain two lines of text with a limit of 12 or 18 characters per line, depending on the language in which you write your ad.

- With this limitation on space, every word needs to be carefully chosen.

- Remember to include the keywords you have purchased in your ad.

- Include a clear call to action.

- The Web site you are sending the traffic to shows up on the third line, if you want to enter one.

Step 5: *If applicable (100% recommended), select the option that allows customers to connect directly to your business phone.*

This will put a call link next to the Web site.

Step 6: *Drive traffic to a mobile-friendly page.*

Step 7: *Split test with different pages and ads; generate various statistics and analytics.*

Step 8: *Monitor your traffic and your conversions daily, if not two to three times a day.*

Google has a great ad-performance report system, allowing you to track everything you could possibly need. In fact, Google information is so powerful and all-inclusive, you could spend your entire day just looking at the reports (not recommended). You can track things like visitor sources, visitor locations, time on your site, and what pages they viewed. You can even do a site overlay that allows you to see exactly the places your visitors are clicking. In terms of reporting, you can run reports to see whether you are meeting your goals and conversions, as well as general reports to give you a macro-level view of your traffic.

Step 9: *Test, optimize, and repeat.*

As with traditional pay-per-click, you are going to find that there are certain phrases that pull and provide a much better ROI than others. Integrate the words and ads that perform the best and dump those that do not.

Step 10: *Move on to another advertising site.*

You should master one ad site before jumping to Facebook, YouTube, and the others. There are hundreds of places where you can place mobile ads. You will, however, find that steps 2 and 3 will produce the bulk of your ROI (the old 80/20 rule).

Step 11: *You can also sponsor ads on various free games and applications available on smartphones.*

So far, this hasn't been shown to be overly effective. When people are playing free games, they may click on the ad quickly, but immediately exit and go back into what they were doing. When you're in a playing mood, typically you are not in a buying mood! It also can get annoying to see ads when you're just not in the mood to see ads.

Voice Broadcasts

A voice broadcast is simply that: a short recorded message that gets blasted out to hundreds or thousands of people. Typical uses for voice broadcasts are promoting major events or campaigning. Ever get those recorded campaign calls? That's a voice broadcast. Voice broadcasts apply to regular phones as well as mobile phones. Your objective is to use voice broadcasts only when you have good information to convey. Do not use the broadcast just for the sake of using it. Make sure that people are not on the do-not-call lists as well.

Here are some fun uses for voice broadcasts:

- Final reminders, such as attending an event or coming on a webinar
- Special offers
- Product promotions
- Just to say hi

To Do

How to Get Started with Voice Broadcasts:

Step 1: *Sign up for a phone-dialer solution.*

Here are our recommendations:

- www.ringcentral.com
- www.VoiceShot.com
- www.VoiceBroadcasting.com
- www.CampaignCaller.com

Step 2: *Load your phone numbers into the system.*

Make sure that you are adhering to state laws because there are various do-not-call rules and regulations.

Step 3: *Create the audio message adhering to these guidelines:*

- Make sure you sound upbeat and relaxed.

- Clear and concise information will outperform the rest.

- Keep the length to less than 30 seconds.

Step 4: *Let the dialer run its course.*

Most of these systems can dial 1,000 phone calls simultaneously or up to 1,000,000 per day. Yeah, it's pretty crazy.

Voice broadcasts are just that simple. We have used this for our events and have seen the attendance rate climb as much as 20%. We also have associates who have used voice broadcasts as an eleventh-hour effort for an event that was about to flop, and their attendance rate literally tripled! It is simply another means of getting your message across. Because most people have their mobile phones attached to their hips, we prefer to send voice broadcasts only to mobile phones rather than typical house lines. Our listening rate is much higher, and there are fewer people on do-not-call lists for mobile phones.

Mobile is growing faster than any other online-marketing method, tactic, or technique. I've given you the tools to implement; it's now your turn to pick and choose which ones will make the most sense for your business and get them into action. Start by collecting mobile numbers. Then test the waters with a basic SMS campaign. Get a bit more daring with MMS messaging, and then move over to some mobile ads. You could put yourself years ahead of your competition and get the lion's share of the revenue from this great marketing source.

5

Virtual Reality Worlds: The Hows and Whys of This Unique Marketing Universe

Marketing using virtual reality worlds is one of the more advanced Web 3.0 marketing tactics that you can use to generate leads, close business, or even communicate with your team. It also takes the biggest time commitment, requiring the most work and the largest initial expense to get the platform designed. The upside: When put into place, these 3-D worlds can prove to be your most effective lead generator, sale closer, and cost saver.

Let me take a step back now that I have your eyes curious and your full attention. Virtual reality worlds are just that. They are 3-D, Web-based communities that allow interaction among users and devices by way of the Internet.

In general, virtual reality has a variety of uses. The whole intent of virtual reality is to convince you and your mind that you're actually there, alive in this make-believe world. It brings the experience and interaction to life, even though you are behind a computer or another device and not there in person.

Picture this:

- Three-dimensional people walking around, interacting and talking. They don't really exist, but they represent people who do in some way.

- Communication using webcams, headsets, micro-phones, and text chat.

- People from all walks of life and from around the world who might never have met otherwise.

- Houses "decked out" with all the latest electronics.

- The ability to walk around, drive cars, purchase goods and services, and do pretty much *anything* you would do in your actual life.

- A world that seems so real, you start thinking it *is* real.

Sometimes your mind continues to believe that this can't be real, it isn't real, and it's fake. It will take some conditioning of your mind (after you start engaging in these virtual worlds) to understand the concept.

Here are some of the common myths about virtual reality worlds:

- **Everyone is fake or acts fake.** Eighty-four percent of people reported that when they join the various virtual worlds, they create people—avatars—that represent themselves. Yes, that does leave 16% of avatars who are not entirely representative of their true selves. Typically these people make minor adjustments, rather than entire modifications of their real personas.

- **It's nowhere near real life.** Many times this is more like real life than your own real life. People host parties and business events. Attend training. Interview for jobs. Shop. Practice foreign languages. Work in global teams. All virtually.

- **It's only for kids.** The average age across most virtual reality worlds is just over 30.

- **The only thing to do in these communities is play games.** Yes, you can play games, but this is only a small fraction of what's done in these worlds.

Here are the key driving factors to the rise in virtual reality usage:

- People have limited time to be traveling across the country to attend meetings.

- Both consumers and businesses have less discretionary income and much smaller travel budgets.

- Everyone continues to adopt the Internet. This makes the whole virtual world concept seem less "off the wall," so to speak.

- It's user-generated content.

People, businesses, and agencies are continuing to move to using virtual reality worlds because they are tired of traveling, have less money to spend on travel, and are realizing the power associated in these worlds. My motto is, "Essentially everything that can be done in person can be done over the Web using various technologies." This is the concept that people are finally starting to understand. Everything continues to move to the Web. So instead of simply resisting, both consumers and businesses are starting to jump on the bandwagon. An additional factor that has helped the rise of virtual reality worlds is their ease of use. Two to three years ago, you needed to have a very fast computer and connection just to view one of these worlds. Today things open up much more quickly and are much more intuitive.

Check out these examples of some of the different things you can do in a virtual environment:

- Instead of attending that rock concert you wanted to go to, check out the same show in a virtual world. Grab some drinks and snacks, and gather around the computer (the bigger the monitor, the better). You will be able to view the avatars performing live, or in some cases live streaming video from the band's studio.

- Think you need to visit the doctor for a diagnosis? Guess again! Go to the doctor's office online, turn on your webcam, and you're in business. Need some tests run? Your doctor can order a nurse to your house or send you at-home testing supplies!

- Want to fly in your employees for a yearly sales meeting, but don't want to spend the money? Host the same meeting on a site like www.SecondLife.com.

- Need to purchase a new camera? Visit the camera store in one of the various virtual worlds, interact with a salesperson, purchase the product, and have the real thing shipped to your home or office.

- Looking for sales leads? Visit one of the thousands of networking locations on the various sites. These are typically labeled "networking lounges."

Anything you would want to do in person (yes, everything) can be done over the Web in the comfort of your own home or office. Why do you think www.Amazon.com had one of its best holiday seasons ever in 2008, while Circuit City closed its doors? Granted, there were various outside factors as to why Circuit City failed. But from the customer's perspective, if I can buy the same products on www.Amazon.com and save time and money (including sales tax and shipping charges in many cases), there is absolutely no need for me to visit a real store, deal with a salesclerk who probably doesn't know what he's talking about, stand in line, and risk having my credit card information misappropriated. And so virtual-reality-world usage continues to climb.

The Basics of Virtual Reality World Communities

Let's switch gears just a bit here and chat about the different virtual communities you can potentially leverage for your business, along with some additional background information to help you understand the lingo a bit better.

There are various common threads among most virtual worlds:

- Typically they are run by user-generated content rather than people at the particular company adding content.
- Users can purchase and own virtual land.
- Currency can be exchanged and typically needs to be converted.
- There are various e-commerce applications and functionality, so you're able to buy products and services in real time.
- They are regulated to comply with the various real international laws.

Here are some of the virtual-world terms you should be aware of:

- **Avatars:** The term is derived from Sanskrit and relates to a "mental traveler" in Indian fairy tales. In the virtual world, it is the character you use to represent yourself and communicate with others.
- **Community:** The people or residents who inhabit the virtual space.

- **Currency:** Most of the virtual worlds have their own form of currency, which typically can be converted into USD or other forms of real money.

- **Emotes:** These express emotions in a virtual world (laughing, crying, smiling, and so on).

- **Grid:** The technology and platform behind the virtual world.

- **Latency:** The lag of movements in motion. It's measured in the delay of the actual change of position versus the response time. The faster your computer and Internet connection, the lower the latency you will experience.

- **Teleport:** To fly to another location in the virtual space.

- **Universe:** The collection of all entities and the space they are embedded in for a virtual world. Each virtual reality site has its own "universe," so to speak.

There are hundreds of popular virtual communities and worlds with thousands of users in existence that are much less popular. Let's zero in on the most popular ones that you need to be concerned with.

www.SecondLife.com

Let's start with the community that has received the most media attention. www.SecondLife.com does not have the largest number of registered users, but it has received more media coverage than most of the other major players because it has poured money into PR and also has had some notable people use the site.

Second Life was launched in June 2003 by Linden Labs. It allows its residents to interact with each other, socialize, conduct business, and so on, across its grid. You must be 18 or older to use Second Life, and between the ages of 13 and 18 to use Teen Second Life. This is an important distinction for marketing purposes to know that users are 18 and older. Second Life has more than 15 million registered users.

Registration is free for personal use. If you want to purchase land, there are monthly fees ranging from $5 to $295 per month, depending on the amount of space you are looking to purchase. For $295, you can have your own private island. A big advantage of purchasing land is that you can start controlling the marketing space. Most of your competitors will not be on these virtual sites. Get your land before they do.

Much as in the other virtual worlds that will be outlined next, currency can be exchanged. In Second Life, the currency used is Linden dollars. The exchange rate from Linden dollars to USD and other currencies varies based on market factors—buy and sell rates.

There have been live concerts in Second Life, government embassies established, and education and training going on pretty much 24/7, to name just a few of the applications. Keep a close watch on this virtual reality world, because it has the most potential for continued and massive growth.

www.ActiveWorlds.com

Active Worlds is a little different from the rest. It is a 3-D world platform with a browser that runs on Windows. (Yes, this helps Bill Gates's wallet grow even larger!) Originally, Active Worlds' programmers wanted to integrate a 3-D browser. Think of Firefox or Internet Explorer in 3-D. Instead, it has morphed into another Second Life.

For consumers, they can play around with their avatar in one of the 1,000 different worlds across the platform, interacting with each other, playing games, or purchasing goods and services.

For businesses, this has been a solid platform on which to develop buzz, sell products, support customers, and provide demos and training.

The advantage of www.ActiveWorlds.com over www.SecondLife.com is that the cost to develop a presence is easier and much less expensive. (To develop a full-blown store on www.SecondLife.com, you are looking at upwards of $5000 to $10,000 or more.) Your time to market on www.ActiveWorlds.com will be much quicker than on www.SecondLife.com. They also are very business-centric. They understand that virtual-reality-world marketing is growing in popularity and have catered many of their offerings and support to businesses while making it effortless for consumers to buy. They are trying to bring the www.Amazon.com experience to their virtual world!

Entropia Universe

Entropia Universe is in a different league than the rest because it has a real cash economy. Some consider this a good thing, others do not. Entropia Universe is an online, 3-D, virtual universe for entertainment, social interaction, and trade, using a real-cash economy. The virtual world was developed by the Swedish software company MindArk, based in Gothenburg. What MindArk really understands is monetization. Instead of charging a subscription price, they use a micropayment model, asking people to buy in-game currency (the PED), which, in turn, can be exchanged back to USD.

MindArk claims to offer the first virtual universe with a real-cash economy. They want people coming to the site to spend money, rather than just to play around. And this is stressed across their Web site and promotional materials.

Entropia Universe has been quite busy attracting various businesses and even government entities. In May 2007, they were chosen by the Beijing Municipal People's Government endorsed online-entertainment company, Cyber Recreation Development Corporation, to create a cash-based virtual economy for China. This is *huge* in terms of adoption and possible numbers. They have been working toward creating the largest virtual world ever. Their proposal was accepted over many others, most notably Second Life. This was a blow to Second Life because they probably assumed that they were the front-runner! Entropia Universe has a goal to attract 150 million users from around the globe. Even more impressive, they expect to generate over $1 billion annually in commerce.

This is not the go-to place for business meetings, however. Instead, it has been a good place for entrepreneurs to sell their e-commerce products and services to consumers and businesses. But, to date, they have some new plans in the works to make the site less gaming-intensive and more cen-tered on business. Check out the site for free and get a feel for it, but don't make a major investment of your time or money just yet.

www.There.com

www.There.com is an online getaway where you can hang out with your friends and meet new ones, all in an abun-dant 3-D environment. It is among the simpler platforms. It currently boasts around one million members, and it has hosted some pretty recognizable stop-bys from people like Yellowcard, The Beastie Boys, Korn, and MIMS, along with events like races and concerts on its platform.

www.There.com also has a cool tool called ThereIM (nice play on words, huh?). ThereIM allows you to communicate with other ThereIM users, but without the need to be logged in to the www.There.com virtual world. The technology is similar to instant messaging. The advantage is that you can still use your avatar to communicate with people, so it's not simply texting back and forth.

A lot of commerce and business is taking place on this platform, because it's less crowded and a bit easier to use. As the membership continues to increase, the number of islands created and amount of business being done on these islands will increase, as well.

www.Kaneva.com

Kaneva is one of the newer players in the 3-D virtual reality space. Kaneva's virtual world came onto the scene in beta form back in 2006. Originally, the vision was to develop a space for game developers to collaborate with each other. Its founders noticed the social-marketing trend moving toward 3-D spaces, so they shifted their vision a bit, though Kaneva still maintains the game platform for the developers, as well.

There are more than 1.4 million users and more than 25,000 communities on their site. The numbers don't come close to those of some of the major players, but their membership has been on the rise, along with their traffic.

Kaneva combines the social-networking aspect and a virtual world with the focus on commerce and entertainment. It's a much more laid-back, fun environment than many of its competitors. What is interesting is that each new member gets a Kaneva City Loft—their own 3-D space. They can tweak their space and furnish it with their own unique style using virtual furniture and accessories.

www.Worlds.com

Having a presence since 1994, www.Worlds.com has been able to grab some significant market share while perfecting its technology. It has proprietary technology along with quite a few strategic partnerships such as Pearson, Time Warner, Hanson, and even the New York Yankees. This allows the company to combine the best of both worlds (no pun intended). It brings excellent graphics, text chat, voice chat, video, and e-commerce to its platform. In the 3-D communities, visitors can interact, visit different worlds, and connect with one another.

www.Worlds.com is very similar to www.SecondLife.com. One key difference, however, remains that www.Worlds.com really did pioneer the technology and the social networking aspect of 3-D communities well before it started to become mainstream. Its site is easy to navigate, making it a must-adopt virtual world in your marketing activities! To top it off, they are fully committed to charity and outreach throughout the world. For that, they get an extra thumbs up!

Moove

The Moove site allows you to create a room, create groups, and chat via instant messaging with a 3-D spin. It's currently a smaller site with just over one million members. Put Moove toward the bottom of your list of sites to leverage, but keep it on your radar. This virtual site would appeal to people targeting a younger audience.

www.IMVU.com

I saved this one for last because it is not a traditional virtual 3-D world. Instead, IMVU is more of an instant-messaging service, forum, and chat room with the 3-D twist. It was founded in 2004 and has since won numerous awards. IMVU is an online destination for people of all ages to meet each other in 3-D. There are plenty of people to meet; they host more than 35 million registered users.

Members of IMVU have fun meeting new people with similar interests and expressing themselves through personalizing their 3-D avatars, digital rooms, music, and home pages. Users also devote time to customizing their individual home pages, setting up public and private rooms, and creating and participating in user groups. These groups are very similar to forums and chat rooms.

IMVU also maintains the world's largest digital-goods catalog, with more than three million items! This has contributed to their bottom line of making $1 million-plus per month from the Web site. The only key difference between IMVU and the more traditional worlds is that you're not flying around a virtual space and visiting different islands and communities. Again, you're using 3-D chat and participating in different groups that have 3-D scenes.

Because this one sets itself apart from the rest, I wanted to provide some specific information geared toward just this virtual world.

To Do

How to Market Using IMVU:

Step 1: *Visit www.IMVU.com and sign up for an account.*

Step 2: *Choose your avatar and username.*

- Make your avatar representative of your personality.

- Because social marketing is meant to be a bit less formal and is focused on building relationships, it's recommended that you keep your profile personal in nature.

Step 3: *Link your address book to the virtual world* (if using Gmail, AOL, Yahoo!, or Hotmail).

Step 4: *Show the real you.*

Load up your profile with some personal and business information. Make sure you include a variety of your interests to spark some interesting chats.

Step 5: *Decorate your room.*

Your room is basically like your own little space where you can invite others in.

- Get creative with your room, and make it match your unique style. I decked mine out for a fun section, as well as a business area that was more formal.

- Use your credits to purchase fun things to add to your room.

Step 6: *Find people.*

This tool is similar to the search functions of social networks like Facebook, MySpace, Friendster, and so on.

- What is amazing about the system is that you can search for people in certain locations, by age, what they are looking for, friends, chatting, networking, and so on.

- When you find someone you would like to chat with, view the person's profile and select Invite to Chat. This will transport you both back to your room for some informal chatting.

Step 7: *Build out your home page.*

Much as with AIM profiles, IMVU builds you out a home page and autopopulates it with some standard information such as name, age, and location.

- Add the rest of the information to make the page complete. I like to write on here exactly what I'm looking for: networking and chatting.

- Keep in mind that it also links to your room, so make sure your room is ready with different furniture and accessories so that you appear to be a bit more advanced than a newbie.

Here is the link to my page for you to check out:

www.imvu.com/catalog/web_mypage.
php?user=38994879

Step 8: *Browse the various groups and join in!*

- This is where the bulk of your business networking will take place (in groups).

- Start off by visiting www.imvu.com/groups to see all the different groups, but don't get overwhelmed by the large number (more than 100,000).

- Zero in on a group or two where your target market will be hanging around. For example, there is a group called Entrepreneurs. I joined the group and instantly began to contribute.

- Groups are very similar to Web forums and the tactics are similar, as well:

    - Contribute some great content. As with the old saying, people don't care how much you know until they know how much you care.

    - Reply and post to different threads.

    - Find and friend people of interest. You're building your 3-D world!

Step 9: *Check out the different live chat rooms, and pick some of interest.*

- There are typically around 25,000 live chat rooms at any given time across IMVU.

- Check out the names for topics of interest.

- After you're in the chat, start a conversation and learn about the different people there.

- If you find people of interest, click on their avatar and select Add to Friends List.

This is much like "friending" across different social marketing Web sites.

On a final note, this can get addicting. In fact, I'm on the site now trying to multitask between work and play. Be selective about whom you talk to and what groups you join. Join groups of which you can be a contributing member; don't just join groups for the sake of joining (or with the idea of just marketing your services or products). Used effectively, this Web site (along with the other virtual worlds) can be a major marketing weapon!

Other Worlds

Here are some of the smaller and less "business like" virtual reality worlds:

- **3D Planets:** This is an online community with excellent 3-D worlds, homes, and jobs. You can move around from the planets, own a home, have a job (complete with a title), shop at the mall, buy and sell items, and earn planet bucks and experience points for using the site.

- **3DEE Virtual Reality:** Would you like to meet people from all over the world and chat with them in an online city? You can move around, communicating in a 3-D cyberspace, all from the comfort of your home on your personal computer.

- **Arounder:** Arounder offers virtual tours of various locations in the world. You can travel in 360 degrees via QuickTime VR—virtual reality—in full-screen panoramas.

- **Avalon:** This is a premier multiuser, role-playing, online-game world.

- **Chamber of Chat:** This is an MMORPG (massively multi-player online role-playing game) graphical experience. It has a number of areas, giving users the feeling that they are actually interacting in a 3-D world. You can hang out with people (students), chill in the common room, network at the pub, play games, and even download sweet wallpapers. The chat feature was created to be a safe place and is monitored by moderators. You must be at least 13 to request a membership.

- **CyberNet Worlds:** This is a 3-D, chat-based program that has your choice of avatar, virtual worlds, file transfer, instant messaging, contacts list, and even the capability to play virtual games in 3-D.

- **Cybertown:** Cybertown is a futuristic, 3-D, family-oriented, cutting-edge, fun, entertainment community with lots to do and see.

- **Disney's Toontown Online:** This is the first massively multiplayer online game designed specifically for kids and families. It is an award-winning, endlessly evolving, kid-safe, immersive 3-D online world.

- **Don Bain's Virtual Guidebooks:** Taking you there using imagery that totally immerses you is what this virtual world is all about, with more than 4,000 virtual reality panoramas of Canada, Alaska, Hawaii, and the western United States.

- **Dotsoul:** Dotsoul is the eternally surreal blog of the online virtual reality world.

- **Euro VR:** This consists of links to QuickTime VRs of the world and Europe and also information on virtual reality. Featured European countries include Austria, Belgium, Denmark, Finland, France, Germany, Greece,

Ireland, Italy, Luxembourg, Netherlands, Portugal, Spain, Sweden, and the United Kingdom.

- **First Age of Avalon:** Experience the power of this realm where it is truly difficult to separate reality from the adventurous life of Avalon, a breathtaking journey into the imagination, where a game is no longer a game, and only you set the limits of what is possible.

- **Full-screen QTVR:** Discover the world in QuickTime Virtual Reality full-screen. Hosted by VRWAY, this is a project of Panoramas.dk and VRMa.

- **Habbo:** Habbo is a virtual world where you can meet and make friends.

- **Hello World! VRMAG:** This is a monthly online travel, photography, and technology magazine that has 360-degree virtual reality panoramas covering great architecture, cities, hotels, resorts, cathedrals, tours, walks, guest columnists, case studies, and feature articles.

- **Karga—The Other World:** This is a 3-D chat system and virtual reality environment where users can move around in 3-D places, talk and see each other, change their appearance, and so on.

- **Mainstreet East:** You can move around in the 360-degree scene of a future street, complete with flying cars.

- **Meez:** You can create animated, 3-D avatars that can be dressed up, as well as play free games and use the avatars in virtual worlds. Your avatar can be used as your AIM emoticon and can also be exported to MySpace, LiveJournal, and other sites.

- **Open Directory Project:** This is the largest, most comprehensive human-edited directory of the Web. It is constructed and maintained by a massive global community of volunteer editors.

- **OuterWorlds:** This is a 3-D multiuser, futuristic chatting system that is available now. Try on an avatar—use a 3-D human figure or some figures that are not so human. Make your avatar wave, dance, and walk. Visit many of the detailed 3-D worlds, interacting with people in real time, from anywhere in the world.

- **Power Pets:** This is an online community/virtual world, where you can adopt (simulated) pets, play games, and meet other simulated-pet owners.

- **TalkTrix Discussion Forums:** These are free-speech forums where you can talk about anything from politics and technology to sports.

- **The Internet TeleCafe:** This is a place to meet new people and make friends from the 30,000-plus active users you can chat with from the TeleCafe. Plus, membership is free.

- **The Palace:** This is the finest avatar-chat community on the Internet. You can download the Palace software, join the online community, and start chatting for free.

- **The World Wide Panorama:** This is part of the Geo-Images Project at the University of California at Berkeley. Check it out.

- **TowerChat:** Create your own customized world, meet new people, and make friends, all within the same online community.

- **Virtual Ibiza:** This is a 3-D gateway world based on hedonism; the island of Ibiza is totally filled with fun. Choose a character and then communicate with like-minded people from all over the globe.

- **Web City Office Towers 3-D World:** This is an ambitious VRML/Web3D-world project consisting of office buildings, places of entertainment, shopping centers, and many other venues. Building doors open to let you in, and you can even use elevators. This world is full of unexpected events and surprises such as music, ATM machines, a theater, and links to other worlds.

- **Whyville:** This is a virtual world targeted to teen and preteen girls and boys. They have 1.7 million registered "citizens" who come from all over to create, learn, and have fun together. Whyville has places to go, things to do, and, of course, people to see. It has its own newspaper, senators, city hall, square, suburbia, economy, museum, beach, and so much more.

How to Leverage the Trend

Now that you know the basics of virtual reality worlds and the different virtual spaces that are getting the most play, let's shift our focus to how to leverage this growing trend. First, let's do a mini-recap of what you have learned about the virtual worlds and look at the advantages and disadvantages of jumping on the virtual train.

Advantages:

- No location barriers
- Demonstrate products in real time
- Awesome user experiences with massive interaction
- Ability to get in touch with peoples' emotions
- Ability to capture market share before everyone else does
- Another sales channel

Disadvantages:

- Not every company will benefit from marketing its products and services in these virtual worlds. If you're a very small company and you intend to stay small, this is not a great space to play in. If you're very locally targeted in your marketing, this will also pose a challenge. Don't expect millions of people to be on these spaces within 20 minutes of your house or office. (But it doesn't hurt to test it out first though, right? This is cutting-edge technology, and you won't know if it doesn't work until you try!)

- It is expensive to build advanced platforms. (So start with the easier-to-use sites that require little to no cash outlay for startup.)

- Expect longer lead times (one to four months). When everything is executed correctly, you should be able to cut down your lead times.

There are so many ways to leverage virtual reality worlds. Check these out:

- **Hosting meetings/events:** Large virtual gatherings are the fastest-growing trend in the 3-D space. Why is there even a need to fly anywhere anymore?

- **Sales calls with prospects:** Why not have your prospect visit your virtual space and chat in a much less formal, yet interactive setting? The content sticks much more than in a traditional call, and seems much more like an actual meeting, rather than a phone meeting.

- **Branding:** People are flying around these portals, so why not have a virtual storefront to brand your products and services?

- **Product launches:** Many people and businesses have announced product launches over TV, on the radio, and even with a press release. Announce a product release in your virtual world to the masses!

- **Demonstrations of your product or service:** Videos are a great way to show a product demonstration, but a live virtual demo is much more powerful (and two-way). Think about how many Snuggies or ShamWows you could sell in a virtual space.

- **Digital product sales:** E-commerce is a huge part of the virtual worlds across the Net. Many of the visitors are prospects browsing for products and services. You might as well have something ready to sell them!

- **Education/seminars:** Teleseminars and webinars are big business. Let's take these events to a whole different level.

- **Training employees/contractors:** Instead of flying people in from around the world, host employee training in your secure virtual space.

- **Live entertainment:** Bands, artists, musicians; think of the potential!

Suzanne Vega, Duran Duran, a U2 tribute band, and dozens, no hundreds, of local celebrity bands are moving from bars and coffee shops to Second Life. Why? It's less intimidating. You can attract a broader range of fans, you can perform at all hours of the day (not just limited to nights and mostly weekends), and you can actually sell tickets and event merchandise.

The crowd? Depending on the time of day and how large the fan base is, a band or performer can have anywhere from a few dozen to literally thousands of people logged in, jamming out to their performance.

A couple more ideas:

- **Charity auctions:** Events go over well in the various virtual communities. Try running an auction to raise money for your favorite charity.

- **Company communication:** Instead of using just plain chat, spice it up with one of the 3-D chats.

Virtual Trade Shows and Events

The trade show industry and the live-event industry in the United States (and the world, for that matter) are very lucrative. The best part is that they appeal to a whole slew of industries, from business, finance, and entrepreneurship to pets, engineering, and food. Think about attending a trade show in general. What are some of the different elements typically in place?

- Booths of varying sizes and shapes
- Sponsors
- Giveaways (everyone loves swag)
- Attendees
- Product/service demonstrations
- Products/services for sale
- Product literature
- Networking
- Entertainment and education

Case Study

HP, one of the world's largest technology providers, decided to test the waters with a virtual trade show. The event was titled The HP Data Protector Virtual Event. It featured ten booths, with four on-demand product demos and webinars. The environment was designed to be lifelike and very rich and engaging. Overall, the event was a great success.

The Results:

- More than 1,300 attendees
- A more diverse crowd because there was no travel cost

- About 3,300 pieces of content downloaded
- Two-and-a-half hours of live interaction on average per attendee
- Substantial cost savings
- A quicker time to market

Comparison Between Live and Virtual Trade Shows

- **Booths of varying sizes and shapes:** This is the easy one because it's the Web. There is plenty of space available, as well as the capability to deck out your booth. In fact, because of the minimal costs, you can do much more than you could afford to do at a physical event.

- **Sponsors:** Most events have sponsors, and virtual trade shows do as well. You can even sponsor the lanyards people wear!

- **Giveaways (everyone loves swag):** Virtual giveaways are easy. Want to give away something tangible? Ask for a snail-mail address and put it in the mail. Send a free report via e-mail. Offer a gift certificate for services and trial samples of your product.

- **Attendees:** What's an event without participants? Visitors can use webcams, text chat, and voice chat, just as if they were there in person!

- **Product/service demonstrations:** Need to show prospects or attendees a product demo? Not a problem. Programmers can make anything happen!

- **Products/services for sale:** We are out to make money, aren't we? You can take credit cards and process orders on the spot!

- **Product literature:** With the click of the mouse, you can send digital files to anyone interested.

- **Networking:** There are plenty of networking lounges in the various virtual trade shows. You can exchange virtual business cards, talk for as long as you'd like, and even drink a glass a beer with a fellow attendee!

- **Entertainment:** Normally, when you're traveling, there are some forms of entertainment. In a virtual space, you may enjoy virtual cocktails along with some music playing in the background.

If you are considering taking trade shows out of your marketing plan, here are some powerful reasons you will probably produce better results by going virtual:

- It's better for the environment. Unisfair, the virtual trade-show host, has saved its clients almost 162,000 tons of carbon dioxide emissions.

- There's no physically draining setup and breakdown. You can literally "assemble" your virtual booth in less than an hour, and it can be saved for the next show.

- It's cheaper than sending your entire sales and marketing staff. You might actually be able to cut some full-time sales jobs if those people spend a lot of their time on the road going to these conferences.

Plus, with no travel needed, not only are you doing your part to help the environment, but think of all the time that will be better used than sitting in an airport terminal waiting for the next flight to come in. It's a win-win for everyone.

Advantages of Virtual Trade Shows

Virtual trade shows have quite a few advantages over live, in-person shows.

- **Huge cost savings for both the vendors and the attendees.** This is the main reason more of these keep popping up.
- **Potential for more staff.** It's easier to have people staff a virtual booth than it is to have them staff a real one.
- **Higher likelihood of people keeping product literature.** More often than not, people go back to their hotel rooms and throw out your expensively produced literature. If the documents are virtual, they are much easier and more convenient to store on a hard drive so that it can be easily found when it's needed.
- **Higher attendance.** With the high cost of travel, more people are flocking to virtual trade shows.

Disadvantages of Virtual Trade Shows

Although virtual trade shows have some great advantages over physical trade shows, hosting strictly virtual-only shows has a few disadvantages:

- **Not face-to-face.** Many say "belly-to-belly" is still the best route.
- **Multitasking.** You're hoping people give you their full attention, but chances are they may be multitasking.
- **Technology issue.** For the less technologically inclined, virtual worlds may be tough to pick up quickly.

To Do

How to Have a Successful Booth at a Virtual Trade Show:

Step 1: *Prepare for this as if you were preparing for a live event.*

Do not skimp on this event because it's virtual. Think about the extreme cost-to-spending savings you've got coming your way, and preemptively reinvest some of that into your virtual booth.

Step 2: *Use a mind map to plan out your booth and your strategy.*

Set up the booth dimensions, lighting, features, product offers, and all the typical trade show-related items. Before you approach a company to design your booth, know what you want and your expected outcome. When I've helped plan a trade show, I have crafted giveaways, contests, and entertainment to drive traffic to the booth. While there, I also made sure that we had ample product and service literature to give away that was tailored to the event.

Step 3: *Find a virtual trade show to attend that will appeal to your target market, and one that is well marketed.*

Here are some Web sites that list upcoming virtual trade shows that you can attend or exhibit at:

- www.GoExhibit.com

- www.optionsXpress.com

- www.Unisfair.com

- www.VirtualTradeShows.net

Step 4: *Engage a company that specializes in setting up virtual-trade-show booths and one that has a proven track record.*

We recommend the following:

- www.Unisfair.com

- www.ProAccess.net

- www.ZeroOneZero.com

Step 5: *Drive traffic to your booth.*

This should be the easy part! Utilize all the various marketing tactics you are learning to drive as much traffic to your booth as possible:

- Search-engine optimization
- Pay-per-click
- Mobile
- Marketing and cross-promotion in other virtual worlds
- Microblogging
- Press releases
- E-mail blasts to your list
- Sponsorship of the event

Step 5.5: *Use guerrilla marketing tactics to further attract people to your booth after the event has started.*

Some ideas:

- Giveaways
- Contests
- Product demonstrations
- Models (yes, eye candy does work even in the virtual world!)

Step 6: *Have more than enough staff.*

Because this event is virtual, you can make sure that some extra staff members are on hand. Treat this like a physical event. Your staff should be respectful, be dressed accordingly, understand your customers' needs, and be well-versed in any/all product offerings, as well as the intent of the trade show.

Step 7: *Have one staff member hanging out in the networking lounge, chatting with others and drumming up business.*

Tas Tip

This is the key for people attending conferences, as well. The networking lounges are where a lot of deals are getting inked. Yes, it's great to visit the various vendors at their booths, but a lot of deals are done in a more informal setting. Even virtually.

Step 8: *Follow up with the leads quickly.*

What's the use of going to a trade show if you're not going to follow up with the leads? This is the biggest mistake people make after attending trade shows. They do not follow up with the leads.

To Do

How to Start Marketing Using Virtual Reality Worlds:

Step 1: *Select a site you want to start with.*

It's not feasible to develop a presence on all the sites. Start with a smaller site, and then move up to one of the larger ones after you start getting this new world down and become more comfortable in this unique space.

Step 2: *Set up your profile/avatar.*

Much as with social-marketing profiles and forum profiles, you want to be certain your profiles are all-inclusive and representative of your true self. Yes, you can shave a few years off your age and a few pounds off your weight, but be truthful in the rest! Remember, you are trying to generate business, and a professional, yet personal, profile is a must.

Step 3: *Acquire land or space for a storefront if applicable.*

This applies to people who are interested in setting up a shop to brand their product or service or to sell it from a virtual storefront. Second Life allows you to purchase land, while some of the others sell buildings and land. This is a sizable investment, so I recommend setting up a shop if you're a business that is doing at least $1 million per year in revenue.

Step 4: *Build your presence/storefront.*

After you have land or a building, you will most likely need to hire a programmer to help you build out your space. This is where I don't like Second Life and prefer many of the others, like www.IMVU.com. Second Life requires technical expertise to design your storefront and to make it attractive. With IMVU, I get a generic space, but with the push of a button I can change colors, move around plants, buy products to decorate the space, and make it look more like home. There are pros and cons to both. Making your IMVU space look nice will take little cash; however, with a developer, the job can be done quickly. On the other hand, if you have land and can afford a programmer, the sky is the limit.

Step 5: *Network in the various communities.*

Treat virtual worlds like real life. Visit groups, chat rooms, and locations you would frequent in real life. Strike up conversations; you will be amazed as to where things can go. Virtual-reality-world marketing is very similar to social marketing; it simply takes things up a few notches because there is a more visual interaction. Make sure you have all the latest and greatest technology to communicate with people.

Step 6: *Drive people to your virtual space.*

It's one thing to have a virtual space, but it's an entirely different thing to have a virtual storefront that actually produces revenue! Treat your virtual space as if it were another Web site that needs traffic to succeed. Use your Web marketing tactics to funnel some of your traffic to this space.

Step 7: *Use it!*

This may sound basic, but there are a surprising number of people who go through all the trouble to establish a virtual presence and then do nothing with it. Review the various ways you can use your virtual space (trade shows, sales meetings, employee training, and so on).

Step 8: *Mix things up.*

Keep your space fresh and fun. Keep in mind that trends are constantly changing and the technology is becoming more affordable. Staying on top of the latest trends will help your virtual space stand out from the crowd.

Step 9: *Constantly track your ROI.*

This can become a time-consuming process. Many of our clients have a full-time employee who is 100% dedicated to maintaining and networking on their various virtual worlds. Virtual worlds are not for every business. Before you invest a lot of time and energy in this marketing tactic, set up the analytical measurements to make sure you can track your efforts.

Virtual-Reality-World Banner Ads

Traditional banner ads are just dandy, but people often view them very quickly and click on them without looking. People are jumping to a different Web site every 34 seconds on average, so most such ads have a negative ROI.

Place some advertisements across a few of the different virtual spaces.

Because only some of the sites allow advertising, and policies differ from one to the next, I will not be giving you a step-by-step how-to list. Instead here are some guidelines:

- Split-test a few different ads.
- Make sure that the people viewing them are targeted.
- Track and monitor statistics to ensure a solid ROI.
- Commit to no more than a two-month campaign, and set your budget relatively low.

With the rate of people flocking to virtual worlds increasing daily, there is no reason you should ignore this Web 3.0 marketing tactic. It's an awesome way to connect with people on a deeper level without having to bear the crazy travel costs. When you really take a step back and see how this fits nicely into your marketing, it can be a game changer. Virtual-reality-world marketing still has a long way to go before it will be considered mainstream, but that is probably the most exciting part. If this were mainstream, you would already be too late! See you in the virtual world!

6

Video Marketing: Taking Video to the Next Level

The Video Craze

There is no doubt of the huge video craze across the world. Everything has been shifting from text and audio to video. We want to *see* things rather than just *read* or *hear* them. The social-proof factor ("hey, I saw it instead of just reading it"), entertainment factor, ease of use, and ability to find pretty much anything online continues to drive the video market and its popularity.

One major shift that has occurred is the shift from physical DVD viewing to the availability of on-demand viewing. If you want something, you typically want it now. You don't want to get in the car, strap the kids in the car seats, and hike down to Blockbuster or the local Family Video store only to find that the movie you wanted to see has been sold out for days. Now you don't have to. With the various subscription services, you can download the movie to your computer or watch a library of movies via your cable or satellite subscriptions.

We are a *now* society, especially when it comes to entertainment. This is one of the many reasons YouTube has become such a phenomenon. You can visit the Web site and be entertained for hours with videos on everything from concerts, comedy scenes, and home videos, to teenagers acting crazy, firework displays, and worldwide news.

What really has made YouTube popular is the fact that it is user-generated content. Want to become an instant movie star? Grab a video camera, start shooting, push a button, upload your video, and forward it to your entire e-mail address book. If the content sticks, it very well may go viral. Let's pause for a moment and look at a case study on viral videos.

Case Study

The free-hugs campaign is among my favorite of the viral videos on YouTube. The video starts off with a tall guy (with some pretty crazy long hair), Juan Mann, walking around town with a sign that says "FREE HUGS." For the first 49 seconds of the video, no one gives him a hug; people just look and stare. Finally, an older lady gives him a hug, and the video turns from black-and-white to full color.

As the video progresses, dozens of others give him hugs—people of different shapes and sizes. He even lets a few others borrow his sign to attract more people. Two minutes and 30 seconds into the video, the free-hugs campaign is banned. What they didn't mention in the video is that the police said the man needed $25 million of insurance to continue.

So what does he do? He calls the media stations and gets a petition going so that he can continue the free-hugs campaign. They gathered more than 10,000 signatures, and the campaign was reinstated. The video has received nationwide attention and accomplished its goal. Keep reading to see what the goal actually was. I'll give you a hint: It was not to jump-start a movement.

Visit www.marketinginthemomentbook.com and click on the viral videos link for the link to this video.

The Result:

- Over 57 million views to date

- Nationwide attention and press, including *The Oprah Show*

- A record deal for the band "Sick Puppies"

The Takeaway:

- If you get a viral topic, let it spread.

- *Things are not always what they seem.* Most people didn't realize that the intention of this video was to get the band a record deal, not to simply give free hugs, despite what the creators may say.

- Never underestimate the power of video.

The video craze has also continued to grab some traction for other reasons. First, you're able to watch programs you might have missed on TV through video sites. Many stations, like NBC, make the episodes of their shows available for viewing online. *The Office* gets millions of views. If you're at work and need to catch up on the latest episode, feel free to do so! Hopefully this sentence doesn't cost corporations billions of dollars in lost productivity (that they are losing now anyway due to video watching).

Anything and everything you're looking for is there. If you can think of it, chances are there are videos about it, especially on YouTube. Much of YouTube is organized into channels:

- Autos & Vehicles
- Comedy
- Education
- Entertainment
- Film & Animation
- Gaming
- Howto & Style
- Music
- News & Politics
- Nonprofits & Activism
- People & Blogs
- Pets & Animals
- Science & Technology

- Sports
- Travel & Events
- Comedians
- Directors
- Gurus
- Musicians
- Non-Profit
- Partners
- Politicians
- Reporters
- Sponsors
- Shows
- Movies
- Contests
- Events

To Do

How to Take Advantage of Online Video:

Before I jump right into the video switch that is being made, I wanted to give you a few tips on how to make sure you're capitalizing on static video, mainly the videos that you continue to see popping up on sites like YouTube and Facebook.

Step 1: *Decide what outcome you want to achieve with the video.*

Choosing some topics with your objectives in mind is much easier than picking topics to see whether they can fit. Here are some ideas of what your marketing purposes might be:

- Build general buzz and branding

- Sell products and services

- Boost search-engine rankings

- Educate the marketplace

Step 2: *Buy some hardware.*

Purchase some video equipment based on the amount of video you plan to shoot and the quality you want to produce for your target audience.

- I keep things simple with a Flip Camera (which I'll discuss later in this chapter), Sony video camera, and lights.

- Other people have green screens, teleprompters, high-end lighting, microphones, and much more.

It comes down to your use. For everyday use, simple equipment is fine.

Step 3: *Shoot your videos.*

I prefer to use settings other than an office. You will find videos of me and my team on airplanes, at parks, on boats, and even at fast-food restaurants. The trick with shooting videos is to make them stick. This is why we shoot in unique landscapes. Talking about marketing can be dull. Relating marketing to Big Macs spices it up a bit!

Step 4: *Edit the video, as needed.*

I prefer to do very light editing, if any at all. Rougher-cut videos are better perceived by prospects and do a better job of creating relationships with your viewers.

- Intro

- Outro

- Add your unique landing page link at the bottom of the video

- Music

- Adjust lighting and sound if needed

Step 5: *Set up video accounts with some of the major players:*

- YouTube

- Vimeo

- MySpace

- vSocial

- VideoEgg

- Dailymotion

- Brightcove

Step 6: *Sign up for a service like www.TubeMogul.com or www.TrafficGeyser.com.*

These tools will allow you to submit your videos to multiple places at the same time. TubeMogul is free, whereas Traffic Geyser is a paid service. Traffic Geyser continues to add new services and tools to help you take full advantage of your videos.

Step 7: *Use video everywhere.*

Here are some examples:

- On your home page as a welcome video

- As a press release

- To describe a product and your services

- On thank-you pages

- To gather opt-ins

- For FAQs

- As video walk-ons (a person appearing on the user's screen)

Step 8: *Get your video ranked in the top of the search engines.*

Google loves video. It's one thing to get your Web site ranked in the top of the search engines, but it's another thing to get a double ranking with your business occupying two spots. To do this, simply do the following:

- Shoot a great video on a controversial topic.

- Upload the video to YouTube.

- Insert keywords into the title, tags, keyword tags, and description.

- Write at least 25 articles and blog posts that also contain the keywords and point them back to the YouTube page, not your Web site. When you have a large number of links pointing to the video, Google sees it as a more popular page and ranks it higher.

Tas Tip

This tactic alone will get you massive traffic. Having double search-engine rankings will drastically increase your natural/organic search-engine traffic.

Make sure you are tracking your video results. For example, if you have a cooking video on how to cook the perfect turkey, include a link in the video to a specific landing page that you set up like this: *yourdomain*.com/turkey. You can then check the traffic of that specific page to see whether the video generated any traffic, opt-ins, or sales.

Online video will continue to become more and more popular and powerful. Google recently changed the way it ranks Web sites (search-engine optimization) and now includes code to accommodate video. This was a huge step in the right direction. As video becomes easier to use, less expensive, and more called for, you will see exorbitant numbers of businesses and people using video in their marketing (if they are not already doing so).

Shifting from YouTube to Ustream and Beyond

At this writing, YouTube has 71 million unique visitors a month. But a site called Ustream.TV will take your Web marketing 3.0 efforts to a new level. I'm talking about watching events and videos *as they happen*. Want to watch a viral video? Join the channel and watch as it unfolds. Want to get involved? Take part in some live user interaction during the viewing!

Tas Tip

It's all about the user interaction. This goes for everything: user-generated content, webinars, video, virtual worlds, mobile marketing. The key take-away with these concepts is to make sure that the users can get involved. How fun is it to sit and watch? Depending on what it is, it can be fun. Want to make it more fun and turn it into an experience? Get the users involved. This concept is so important, I may just end the book right here....Okay, you got me, I'll continue.

Two Options for Viewing Video

When boiled down, there are really only two options for viewing or watching video online:

Option 1: You can watch a video presentation on how to roast a marshmallow on YouTube.

Option 2: You can view a stream-broadcasting at 9:30 PM at my house in my backyard as I demonstrate, live, how to roast a marshmallow.

Which option do you prefer? Option 1 is great for busy people who can't make the time, but most will go with Option 2 so that they can be a part of the event. To facilitate the interaction, I can ask others to roast marshmallows and show their live feed, take questions over the phone, or take questions over chat. During the event, I will also be tweeting, and asking people to retweet to generate additional buzz and interaction.

Advantages of live video:

- Involves user interaction
- Typically brings higher attendance
- Allows viewers to share the thrill
- Appeals to the different senses and emotions

Disadvantages of live video:

- Can bring up scheduling issues
- Involves some lag time, meaning that quicker computers and Internet connections are preferred

As we have done with the other disadvantages, we can provide a rebuttal. If people can't attend your live stream, they can still replay it. The advantage of this over YouTube is you still get some of the live experience on your computer.

In regard to having faster computers and Internet speeds, this used to be the case for most feeds. There was always a delay and some lag time. This situation has improved greatly and will continue to get better as computer speeds, Internet connections, and the actual streaming-video technology improve.

What factors are causing the live-video trend to increase?

- People love to be entertained.
- It is easy to use.
- The usage of the Internet continues to skyrocket.
- On-demand is no longer enough; people want that experience.
- Travel costs are rising.
- People now have the ability to view and capture video from a mobile device.

Let's talk about mobile for a bit. You read the mobile chapter and understand that it's the fastest-growing trend talked about in this book (and Web 3.0 marketing tactic around). Take it a step further. You can stream video live from your iPhone or Nokia S60 cellphone directly to Ustream.TV. Think of the power here. You can report on the latest news and stream video from anywhere in the world with the push of a button! You don't need any fancy video equipment, a makeup artist, a sound guy, or a lighting crew; you simply need your mobile phone. In the next two to three years, most, if not all, mobile phones will have this capability to link up with the various live video-stream sites.

Tas Tip

I've been using the word *trend* a lot in this book. Note the difference between a trend and a fad. Trends are backed by statistics; fads are things that come and go.

There are limitless ideas for using live streaming video in your marketing and branding. Check out these ideas, hot off the press:

- **Conferences:** Virtual worlds are great, but they assume you will be hosting the event solely in a virtual world.

Let's take an example. You are a motivational speaker, hosting one of your semiannual events on how to get yourself motivated in a down economy. A real "upper" topic, huh? The last two words, *down economy*, are going to deter a lot of people from flying in and attending your event. Rather than missing out on all that business, stream the feed live for a fraction of the cost of a live event. Your attendance rate will skyrocket, and you're not limiting yourself solely to people who will physically attend.

 ## Case Study

When Michael Jackson died, millions wanted to view his memorial service, and probably for the first time in history, people signed up for tickets to attend a memorial service. However, only so many people would get to go because of a limited number of tickets and travel restrictions. In the past, we would have been limited to viewing the service on television sets, but not in today's world. Here are just a few statistics of Internet viewers and the Jackson memorial service:

- CNN had more than 9.7 million people view its live stream.

- Facebook had more than 300,000 view its live stream.

- MSNBC had 19 million viewers on its live stream.

- Ustream had more than 4.6 million viewers.

- The United Kingdom's BBC News site had 410,000 live Internet video streams.

The Key Takeaway: If people can't be there physically, they will find a way to take part in some respect.

More than 21.3 million people viewed the inauguration of President Barack Obama, but not from their TVs; they viewed it live from their computer monitors. No, your business event is not going to generate this kind of traffic, but imagine if you sell tickets to attend your event via Ustream for a fraction of the price of a live attendance. People will get all the information they would have gotten if they traveled to the event. (They just miss out on the great in-person networking.) To combat this limitation, offer a networking session on one of the virtual-reality-world sites afterward!

Think of all the people who walk away from the sales table or click off your Web site because they can't afford to come to your event or the date conflicts with their schedule (remember, with a live stream, you can record it to be viewed later). Now think of those same people being converted! Streaming events have huge revenue-building potential.

- **Product/service launches:** What better way to tell the world about a new product or service offering than by announcing it live to your listeners, and taking orders on the spot (think of the Home Shopping Network on the Web).

- **Concerts:** Stream your concert for free or for a small price for raving fans who want to watch you but can't attend.

- **Parties:** Just reached a business milestone and want to celebrate with your staff? Get on Ustream, toast each other, and drink some bubbly!

- **Interviews:** Interviews are a great way to interact. Ustream was used widely in the recent election by both candidates.

- **Education:** Most people on Ustream use the service to educate their viewers on different topics of interest and combine chat with Q&A in the process. An example would be me hosting an informal session on Web 3.0 marketing. For the first ten minutes, you would see me speaking, and for the next ten, I'd take some Q&A.

- **Charity:** Various events and stunts have been hosted on Ustream (and others) to raise money for charity, from sleeping strikes, to playing the guitar for tips, and even all the way to playing video games for 50-plus hours.

- **Chatting/Q&A session:** Looking for the ultimate interaction? Host a chat session with your viewers, taking questions live on the spot! Take it up a level by allowing the person asking the question to be seen on his or her webcam.

 ## Case Study

The Jonas Brothers recently conducted a Web chat to announce some new songs, to show video clips from music videos to be released, and to just chat with their fans. The event was widely successful from all fronts!

The Jonas Brothers result (per a Ustream press release):

- About 1.5 million unique posts were made via Facebook's live feed.

- There was an average of 23,000 posts per minute.

- More than 100,000 users joined the webcast after seeing their friend's comment on Facebook.

- About 974,000 total unique viewers watched the one-hour webcast.

- Ustream reported that the Jonas Brothers webcast on Facebook surpassed the largest live-video event they have hosted for any music artist.

- More than 40,000 tweets were sent out about the event during the one-hour webcast.

The Takeaways:

- Live streaming video is amazing and much more dynamic!

- There is no way you would get the same results by simply submitting the video statically.

Take note of these live streaming video sites:

- www.Ustream.TV
- www.Stickam.com
- www.Justin.tv
- www.Camstreams.com
- www.blogTV.com

Keep in mind, these tactics and steps apply across the board to the others with slight variations. I have zeroed in on Ustream.TV, as you can tell by the title of this section. It sounded a bit catchier than the others. I recommend that you start off by leveraging Ustream.TV because it's the easiest to use and gain traction with.

To Do

How to Market Using Ustream:

Step 1: *Go to Ustream.TV and set up an account.*

- Use your brand as the name of the channel or use something creative to stand out from the crowd.

- Invite friends via Hotmail or Gmail. Link your various accounts (Twitter, Facebook, etc.).

Step 2: *Purchase needed video equipment.*

I simply sport a high-end Logitech webcam.

Step 3: *Connect your webcam or video camera to your computer.*

Step 4: *Create a show.*

- Type the name of the show—for example, Web 3.0 Marketing Tactics.

- Upload a logo (use your logo, or have one created).

- Select the best category that fits with what your show is about. I selected How-to: Business.

- Add some tags. These are keywords people might be searching for and words/phrases that relate to your topic—for example, Web 3.0, Web 3.0 Marketing, Internet Marketing, Web Marketing.

- Write a description. You must make this compelling or people won't watch the show. Think of your description as something you would read to decide whether to watch a movie or a show.

Start 5: *Save the show for later.*

You don't want to broadcast just yet!

Step 6: *Market the show so you get some attendees.*

- Announce it in your other social sites and use other Web 3.0 marketing tactics.

- Emphasize the fact that it's live video with interaction.

- Post it on the various free sites that allow event postings.

- Try to get featured on the home page of Ustream.TV. This is done by submitting a request far in advance to Ustream.TV. Send the request to events@ustream.tv and include your channel URL, event date, location, and the Internet connection upload speed (which can be tested at Speedtest.net).

Step 7: *Deliver a solid performance.*

- Give away great content.

- Keep it interactive.

- Take questions and feedback.

- If the show is prerecorded, I like to take questions ahead of time and play them as if they were live.

Step 8: *Have a call to action.*

What do you want people to do when they come on your show? If your shows are totally informational, that is what your viewers will expect. And, without a call to further action, your interaction with your viewers could end with the conclusion of your program. That would be a waste of all that effort you just put into the program. So, have a mini pitch or call to action at the end of each show. Here are some ideas:

- Ask viewers to sign up for an additional course with you.

- Offer a reduced price on a training product, if they buy within a certain number of hours or days.

- Invite them to sign up for a member site.

- Offer coaching services.

Whatever your business is, you can gear your pitch accordingly. Just don't get into the habit of constantly providing free information without asking for anything in return.

Step 9: *Use the recording after the live show is over.*

- Post it on Ustream.TV along with the other video sites.

- Give out the recording to your mailing list and other places.

- Even use it on a membership-based Web site where people are paying you revenue each month for unlimited access.

Step 10: *Utilize stats and analytics.*

Check out your stats right in the dashboard area, and then cross-check that with analytics to make sure you're generating some traffic. This allows you to view statistics from two places.

Internet TV

If you got excited when I talked about live streaming video, you're going to love the next unique Web 3.0 marketing tactic even more: hosting your own live Internet TV channel.

Starting Your Own Internet TV Channel

So you've grasped the concept of live streaming video and fully understand the advantages of live versus static videos (like the ones you browse on YouTube). Now, how about having your own, live TV channel that is broadcasting constantly on the Internet?

When most people think of Internet TV, they think of watching their favorite TV shows or various movies. This has been around on the Net for a few years, and the quality continues to get better with the expansion of high definition (HD). Your very own Internet TV channel has a similar general concept. The difference is you're not a huge TV station, and you're not broadcasting movies or soaps. Instead, your channel is going to be educational in nature and will turn into a lead-generating powerhouse.

To further simplify things, think of this example: One of my favorite networks is ABC. If I were to stay up for 24 hours straight, I would see a mix of things:

- Prerecorded shows
- Commercials
- Live shows, like the news

Your Internet TV channel will be similar in that broad view. You are going to offer some prerecorded materials, host some live events, and stock the waves with commercials and sponsors.

Take a look at some of the reasons you would want to have your own Internet TV station:

- Your own Internet TV station positions you as an expert.
- It gives you a great tool to educate your marketplace.
- It's a medium for you to interview people.
- It gives you another sales channel.
- It generates leads.
- You can earn ad revenue through it.
- It gives you the opportunity to have a constant presence in your space, with the freshest, most up-to-date content available.

Many people have grabbed domains ending in .tv. Not surprisingly, .tv is the assumed natural extension for television, and because of this, .tv domains have great marketing appeal.

To Do

How to Start Your Internet TV Channel:

Step 1: *Develop your station mind map so you know where you're headed.*

- What do you want to get out of your TV station?

- What content do you want to provide?

- What will be your hours of operation?

- When will you be live versus prerecorded?

- Create a schedule of events and topics.

Step 2: *Get a domain.*

I recommend getting a domain name just for this endeavor. The .tv domain names have been the most popular for anything related to a TV station. What you need to keep in mind is that .tv does not stand for television. It is actually the extension for Tuvalu, the Polynesian island nation.

Step 3: *Hire a good team to design and code a Web site.*

- It should look like a typical Web site. The difference: In the middle of the screen, there should be a large TV that is streaming your video or broadcasting live.

- Publicize your sponsors.

- Have different sections on your Web site where people can browse your products and services, learn more about you, contact you, and carry out all the other typical options.

- Change your site often to reflect current promotions and features.

Step 4: *Set up a dedicated area for filming.*

Since you will be doing both prerecorded and live videos, you should have an area in your home office (or an off-site office) that is decked out with all the necessary equipment and will look great on film.

Step 5: *Purchase suitable equipment for recording video and broadcasting live.*

You can get all of this for under $2,000:

- An HD camera is recommended.

- Audio equipment: microphone, headset, clipped microphone, or even some wireless audio equipment.

- Lighting: Invest in some great lights.

- Green screens. (These are great because they allow for easier editing of video and still photos.)

- Teleprompter, if you want to read from a script.

- Connect your camera to your computer, and get ready to stream live!

Step 6: *Get a good Web site host that can handle the bandwidth and the constant streaming of video.*

Some good companies include the following:

- www.Rackspace.com

- www.Streamhoster.com

- www.Veeple.com

- www.EndavoMedia.com

- www.TalkPointCommunications.com

Step 7: *Record content you can load onto the station.*

Don't think you need hundreds of hours of content to launch your station. You can start with just a few hours of content. Reread the ideas for the live events in the earlier part of the chapter for content ideas and things you can do live or prerecord.

Here are some other content ideas:

- Webcam broadcasting 24/7 (or in certain hours)
- Other people's content you can use (with permission)
- Old video recordings
- Testimonials from clients and customers

Step 8: *Keep in mind you don't need to have content up 24/7.*

- We have four hours of prerecorded content daily, two hours of live stuff, and some commercials mixed in.
- We let that content repeat for six hours.
- We then have 12 hours where there is nothing more than a Microsoft PowerPoint presentation and some music.

The reason we have done this is that we have found the times when people were browsing the station. There is no reason to put up content if very few people are on your Web site at a given time! If your audience is largely global, and in different time zones, you will want to consider having a larger amount of content at different times.

Step 9: *Host some live events.*

Live events are a great draw, as we talked about previously. The difference is you will be hosting your events on your Web site rather than appearing on someone else's.

Step 10: *Promote your hot new TV channel everywhere.*

And when I say everywhere, I mean *everywhere*.

- Link it on your Web sites, social sites, and beyond.

- Send out multiple press releases using a service like www.PRWeb.com.

- Partner with some other people in exchange for free advertising.

Step 11: *Step it up a notch!*

As your station becomes more popular, you can start commanding various features and money-making opportunities:

- Paid advertising.

- Banner ads on your site.

- High-profile guest interviews. Heck, maybe you will become the next Oprah!

Case Study

The United States, as a society, is pretty obsessed with the news and politics. I recommend you don't get too obsessed, but it's your call! To feed this obsession, the White House released the site www.WhiteHouse.gov/live/. On this Web site, they provide live feeds, offer pre-recorded video sessions, and even have slide shows. This has become the go-to place for White House TV and information.

The Result:

- The site gets millions of monthly views.

- It's a great community builder.

- More than three million Web sites link to the site.

- It gives the White House another medium to reach its constituents.

The Takeaways:

- Having a dedicated portal/site for video is a great idea.

- Both live and prerecorded video content will fare well because people have different viewing habits.

Much as in virtual reality worlds, having your very own Internet TV channel may seem a bit far-fetched, but why not give it a try? Load up a few hours of content, let it rotate, and stream at various times and see what feedback you get. You hold a great advantage if you can also say, "Hi, I'm Mr. Smith. I'm an entrepreneur. By the way, did I mention I have my own Internet TV station?" People gravitate toward experts, and this is another mode to increase your expert status and sell some products and services at the same time. And quite frankly, when you start getting the hang of it, it's rather fun!

The Flip Video Craze

Now that I have you all worked up to be shooting lots and lots of video, I'm going to make your life ten times easier and talk about my favorite video-shooting device.

Let me set the stage. This device:

- Fits in your pocket
- Shoots HD quality
- Is easier to use than a cellphone
- Connects to your computer's USB port in seconds
- Was dubbed one of the most significant electronic products of the year by the *New York Times*
- Costs less than $200

Drum roll, please.... The device: *the Flip Video.*

This device will allow you to record up to 120 minutes of HD-quality video and audio with the push of a button. It is so easy to use, I've purchased it for my relatives who have always told me they are technologically impaired.

You turn it on, push one button to record, push another to zoom, if you'd like, and push one button to stop recording. When you're ready to transfer the video to your computer, you simply push the slider, and out pops a USB connector. Slide the connector into a USB drive in your computer and you're in business!

To Do

How to Jump on the Flip Video Marketing Craze:

Step 1: *Buy a Flip Video camera.*

- I recommend having two. I keep one in my car and one in my office.

Step 2: *Buy some accessories as you see fit.*

- Carrying case

- Tripod stand

- Underwater case

- Extra battery or two

Step 3: *Carry it everywhere you go.*

This is the most important trick when it comes to video. You're going to be out and about and things will come up for which you are going to say, "Darn, I wish I had my camera."

Step 4: *Record lots of video.*

Here are some fun ideas for ways my clients and I have used our Flips (both business and personal):

- Record testimonials

- Create video blog posts

- Produce educational videos

- Promote products

- Capture crazy events when you're out and about

Step 5: *Use the software that comes preloaded on the Flip to lightly edit the videos, as needed.*

We've conducted numerous surveys, and video that is a bit more "raw" has been preferred six times to one. People connect more with you if your videos don't seem staged and are just real footage.

- If publishing these videos across the Web, remember to include your landing-page URL at the bottom of the video.

Step 6: *Post everywhere!*

Publish to your blog, your Web site, YouTube, your TV channel, and everywhere else across the Net!

Flip Videos make shooting video easy and fun. What really keeps me recommending the Flip, over any of its competitors, is its commitment to charity. Check out the link: www.FlipVideoSpotLight.com.

Go buy a Flip camera or two and join in the fun. These devices really do make shooting video an experience!

The sky is the limit when it comes to online video. You can create some massive buzz using static videos, and even create a station and a following using live video. The fact is, video is here to stay, and it continues to increase in popularity while the quality gets better and better. Using any type of video will help your conversions and your traffic, guaranteed!

7

Web Applications: How to Effectively Use Apps in Your Marketing

What Are Web Apps?

An "app" (which is shorthand for "application") is a piece of software that may be found on your computer, on your mobile phone, or across the Web. Originally, all software programs were called "apps." But recently apps have come to be used specifically to refer to the small programs found on iPhones and now other smartphones, Facebook, and Google. They typically help you do something and make your life a little easier in a big way. For example, the iPhone has an application that allows you to put your phone up to the radio (or any type of speaker) to have the app search for and find the name and musician for the song that is playing!

Over the past two years, the development of different apps has been growing at an extraordinary rate. Even more significant is the use of the apps, which is primarily for many of the Web 3.0 sites and marketing tactics we have discussed.

Rather than only talking about the traditional apps in your marketing, we're going to discuss three totally different ways of looking at apps. First, think of the apps for general business use. These apps will make your job easier, create more revenue, and make communication with your prospects and clients easier. Second, think of using apps in your Web 3.0 marketing. These are the apps that can be used for mobile marketing, in targeted forums, in microblogging, and the like. Third, think of apps as a possible lead generator or profit house. Entire businesses are being made solely for developing, selling, or giving away apps.

Tas Tip

Selling apps is one way to generate revenue. But *giving away* apps is an even more powerful way. As we've discussed before, one of the best marketing tactics for generating leads is to offer free stuff, whether it's a whitepaper, a CD/DVD, or an app. Give first, and it will all work out in the end!

Apps for Personal and General Business Use

Back in the introduction, I talked about the rapid-paced world we live in and how, subsequently, people desire information, entertainment, and tools faster than ever. I personally use apps to make my businesses run more smoothly, to keep me productive, and to have some fun along the way.

Here are 19 applications I use on a regular basis:

1. **Amazon Video on Demand:** The service lets you download movies and TV shows to watch on your PC or portable device.

2. **Skype:** Skype is my favorite way to chat via text, voice, and video over my Internet connection—for free!

3. **www.Answers.com:** Looking for answers? This service pulls information from several reference sites to provide answers to all your questions.

4. **Picasa:** This is Google's Web-based photo-hosting service. Users get 1GB of free hosting; images can be uploaded and manipulated using Picasa.

5. **YouSendIt:** Every now and then, almost everyone has a file to send to someone that's too big to e-mail. YouSendIt meets that need via a Web-based service.

6. **BlogTalkRadio:** Broadcast your own Internet radio show!

7. **LogMeIn:** On the road or off-site and need to access your computer remotely? This is the service that will help you access the files you need.

8. **Kayak:** This service scours the Web to help you find the cheapest deals on travel services around the world.

9. **ooVoo:** Looking to chat with several people at the same time on video? This application is great, and I use it daily.

10. **Zoho:** Looking for massive amounts of productivity tools? Check out the apps offered by Zoho.

11. **Woot:** One item for sale each day, and lots of great bargains. They are an online retailer of goods.

12. **Zillow:** Zillow is an online house-buying service.

13. **Veodia:** You can create video recordings with ease.

14. **VoiceThread:** This is a photo- and video-sharing tool. It lets users upload photos, videos, and documents and add voice, text, and video annotations to each slide.

15. **Mint:** Manage your money through the Web for free.

16. **Pandora:** Want to jam out to some great tunes while working? Free streaming music and video tailored to your likes.

17. **Basecamp:** Looking for a solid Web-based project management tool? This tool will make your groups come together and work on large or small projects on the same shared, collaborative space.

18. **Wikia:** Very similar to Wikipedia, but it is a collection of Wikis that can be edited. So it's actually a white-paper service that lets site owners add Wiki elements to their sites and brand them to match.

19. **Remember The Milk:** Ever forget things? How can you not?! This app makes your to-do items and reminders available via Gmail, SMS, the iPhone, Windows Mobile devices, Skype, and popular IM clients.

At this writing, there are hundreds of thousands of apps available, many of them free—which makes them a welcome presence in your customers' lives. As a result, they are also an interesting avenue for Web 3.0 marketing.

Using Apps in Web 3.0 Marketing

Let's look at how to use apps in your Web 3.0 marketing. In these instances of apps, we are looking for software tools, add-ins, and fun programs that help us accomplish a few things:

- Increase the relationship building among your prospects/clients.
- Aid in the experience your prospects/clients receive.
- Make communication easier and faster.
- Help with the fun factor in your marketing.

Apps can be used pretty much anywhere. In the Web 3.0 arena, we're looking at apps that can go along with some of our other marketing tactics to beef up the efforts:

- Microblogging
- Mobile
- Virtual reality worlds
- Live streaming video

Twitter Apps

One of the biggest problems marketers have with Twitter is the challenge of keeping up with the large amounts of tweets and direct messages. This causes a delay in response time, along with the chance of missing some critical information. As a result, Twitter has allowed developers to start building apps to aid in this dilemma—helping Twitter members organize and prioritize the hundreds or thousands of incoming tweets they receive every day.

Visit www.Squidoo.com/twitterapps to view 275 apps you can put to use!

My favorite Twitter apps include these:

- Twitterific
- Google Desktop for Twitter
- TweetDeck
- Tweet Later

The first three apps allow you to manage your tweets, making it much faster to get back to people. Tweet Later allows you to set up an autoresponse that goes out to anyone who follows you, among dozens of other uses.

Mobile Apps

We talked about apps extensively in Chapter 4, "Mobile Marketing: Tapping into Billions of Cellphone Users." There are thousands of apps for use across the most popular devices, including the iPhone and BlackBerry. Many apps allow you to interact more quickly with your Web 3.0 marketing sites. For example, there is an iPhone app that connects to your Twitter account, allowing you to tweet more quickly. You can also shoot a short video or audio with your iPhone and have it tweeted instantly! Take this to another level with Ustream's new live broadcast app. You can view, record, and broadcast live!

Facebook Apps

I don't consider Facebook a Web 3.0 company for one key reason: The site is open to the masses. Remember, one of the key trends in the shift from Web 2.0 to Web 3.0 is the openness of the Web. Consumers are flocking to more exclusive and private social networks rather than simply doing all their networking on Facebook. The site is a powerhouse and generates a lot of revenue for our clients, but the whole point of this book is to talk about the up-and-coming trends and the trends that have already been in play that you don't yet know about. Keep using Facebook, but know that there is going to be a Facebook revolt in the very near future!

Although Facebook is not a Web 3.0 company, there are various apps that can help you use it as a Web 3.0 marketing tool.

Here are my seven favorite apps for use on Facebook:

1. **LinkedIn:** This puts a convenient LinkedIn banner on your profile and a direct link to your LinkedIn profile.

2. **Books:** This app allows people to see what you have read and are currently reading.

3. **Causes:** Become an advocate of your favorite causes and charities, and even raise money right from your profile.

4. **Video:** Upload video right to your profile with ease.

5. **Countdown Calendar:** Use this cool app to have a countdown to anything you'd like, from your birthday to an event you're hosting or even to the New Year.

6. **Where I've Been:** If you travel, this is a must-have. It creates a slick map of the world showing the different places you have traveled.

7. **DivShare:** Sharing MP3s, videos, and other files is a breeze with this app.

Virtual-Reality-World Apps

Virtual-reality-world apps vary across the different virtual worlds. The main thing you need to keep in mind, however, is that virtual-reality-world technology is already very advanced, so most of the apps are already prebuilt into the technology for use. So the capability to add different apps instantly to your virtual worlds is typically nonexistent.

Instead, here are two tactics we use:

1. We use Camtasia or Jing to record our virtual-reality-world presentations. Since these take a lot of prep work, we want to make sure we capture these on camera and then distribute them afterward (typically for a fee) or as a giveaway to capture leads.

2. We always have a direct link to our various virtual-reality-world profiles or links to our upcoming presentations. There are a few apps on sites like Facebook that allow you to do this in an easy and design-appealing fashion. These apps are similar in nature to the LinkedIn app.

Live Streaming Video Apps

With the growing popularity of live video, apps are becoming increasingly available to support that activity. We've used various apps to enhance our users' experiences, but after surveying our users, they actually found most of the apps we used to be distracting to their viewing experience. After testing hundreds, we have settled on two totally different apps that we use on a regular basis:

- **Games:** We broadcast live presentations and shows that often have quite a bit of attendance. What we have found is that many people like to log on early before the broadcast starts. Rather than just having these early birds staring at a blank screen, we have had a few game apps developed to give them something to do beforehand. Our users like the various games we offer, so we continue to develop new, fun games or leverage other game apps already out there.

- **Mobile viewing:** The second type of app we use when it comes to live streaming video is the mobile-viewing and streaming apps. These applications allow our users to view our shows right from their iPhone (or other approved device). They also allow us to stream live video right from our cellphones. You have seen many cellphone-captured videos on YouTube, but I promise you, you have not seen a lot of live footage being broadcasted from a mobile phone. I use my mobile phone to broadcast sparingly because the quality isn't there yet, but it's improving daily.

To Do

How to Start Using Apps to Enhance Your Web 3.0 Marketing Activities:

Step 1: *Brainstorm.*

We like to take a different approach to apps. Instead of first looking at what's out there, we brainstorm on which apps we would like to see and what those apps would do. For example, when we first did this for Twitter, we wrote down more than 40 things we wanted the app to do. Most of the things on that list came back to *"easier management of tweets."*

Step 2: *Search.*

Use my best friend, Google, to find out whether there is an app that meets the criteria you just compiled. More times than not, such an app will already exist.

Step 2.5: *Be innovative.*

If no app is available, keep reading and possibly consider building your own app. There are plenty of developers you can hire. Utilize sites like www.Guru.com, www.Elance.com, and www.craigslist.org. There are thousands of developers at your fingertips.

Step 3: *Reevaluate.*

Make sure that the apps you are installing aid in one (or more) of the criteria we talked about:

- Increase the relationship-building among your prospects/clients.

- Aid in the experience your prospects/clients receive.

- Make communication easier and more effective.

- Help with the "fun factor" in your marketing.

Step 4: *Follow the instructions and install the app.*

Typically, you simply need to be logged in to the particular site, push a button to install the app, and then turn it on or make it live.

Step 5: *Don't get app-crazy.*

Don't install hundreds of apps on your various marketing sites so that all that your prospects and customers see are apps. Make sure your core information is available and easily visible. Limit the apps you use across the different sites to about five to ten, max, per site.

Step 6: *Gather feedback.*

Survey your network to see how users like the apps you are using and whether they have any recommendations. You would be surprised by how few businesses actually use surveys to aid in their marketing. It's a very powerful tool.

Step 7: *Keep an eye out for the bigger and better.*

Keep up-to-date with what new apps become available. I like to use Google Alerts to easily accomplish this task. For example, set a Google Alert for the phrase "twitter apps," and let the Alert tell you when new apps have been developed. Installing and using apps, as you will see, is very straightforward. Just remember that your main purpose is serving your prospects and consumers. If you can't identify a direct benefit to your users, skip it.

How to Create Your Own App

The last key area of Web apps is creating your own applications for marketing uses or to simply sell or give away.

We've done a lot of custom programming and have built out some fun applications for our marketing uses, but we have found that when we have given away apps free, the response was much greater. I mean, let's face it—who doesn't love free stuff?

The key with giving away Web apps is to make the app something of extreme value. The more useful or (if you're taking the other approach) fun it is, the better chance it has of going viral.

Lead Generation and Profit Apps

The main reason people develop apps is to make money from selling them, or they use them as lead generators. For example, a free application that helps entrepreneurs market on Facebook would be a great way to generate a solid list of tech-savvy entrepreneurs.

Some applications we have built in the past include the following:

- Custom applications for aiding in customer service
- Apps for Facebook pages
- A few MySpace apps
- An application for the iPhone
- Several apps to help in lead generation
- WordPress plug-ins/apps

Here are some other ideas of applications you could develop for internal or external uses:

- Expense tracking
- General productivity
- Party planning
- Event management
- Games (people love to be entertained)
- E-mail management

- Music
- Shopping
- Video (streaming or static)
- Mobile

The way we approach application development is as follows:

- We have a 50-minute strategy session in which we're just throwing out ideas. (No idea is bad.)
- We think of apps we would use (or want to play with).
- We check to see whether there is anything similar.
- If we find nothing extremely similar, we build out the app.

And that's it. That is our process for deciding which applications to roll with.

To Do

How to Create Your Own Apps:

Step 1: *Think about it.*

Figure out what you want the app to do, in terms of functionality. Then develop a mind map or a scope.

Step 2: *Decide whether you want to give away the app or sell it.*

Step 3: *Hire a solid developer to build out the app.*

For iPhone apps, we recommend that you check out www.myappcreator.com. You can develop a web app very quickly and deploy it even quicker! They have created apps for celebrities, speakers, authors, and many large brands.

For WordPress plug-ins, check out www.marketinginthemomentbook.com.

Most developers charge between $50 and $250 per hour for their services. If possible, I encourage you to get a flat rate for the app you would like developed. More often than not, you will end up saving money versus an hourly arrangement.

Check out www.Elance.com, www.Guru.com, www.RentACoder.com, and www.craigslist.org for a variety of additional developers.

Step 4: *Set up the lead-capture page to sell or give away the application.*

This step applies more to the giveaway of a free application. If you're going to give something away, you have the right to ask for something in return. In this case, ask for the following information:

- Name

- E-mail address

- Mobile-phone number (remember, *mobile*, not general phone)

- Web site (if applicable)

- A free field for something like comments or how consumers are going to use the app

Step 5: *Price accordingly (if you're selling).*

Keep in mind that a lower-priced product is also a great way to get people familiar with your business. After you get them to say yes the first time, it's much easier the next time!

Step 6: *Drive traffic to your page.*

Remember, this is not an if-you-build-it-they-will-come age anymore. Leverage the Web 3.0 tactics you are learning in this book to drive traffic to your application. If you are driving a lot of traffic to the page but you're still seeing minimal results, take another look at the application that was developed. Is it useful to your target market? Does it have a viral factor to it? Don't just develop applications to give away for the sake of developing applications. If they have solid value to them, you're going to get some downloads and usability.

Step 7: *Create more applications as you see fit.*

What's the best way to figure out which applications to develop next? Do a survey! Use a tool like www.SurveyMonkey.com to survey your audience to see what they would like to see next.

As shown, you have various ways to look at leveraging Web apps in your marketing and in your business. With new social sites, forums, and virtual reality worlds popping up daily, businesses and programmers alike will continue to look at what different apps they can develop. Try out a few of the applications and you will be hooked on apps for life! After you've realized how beneficial apps are, try your hand at developing a few with the intention of their going viral and serving as lead-generating powerhouses!

8

Open-Source Code: How to Find and Use Others' Hard Work for Maximum Impact

What Is Open-Source Code?

Open-source code is a big part of the Web 3.0 revolution because it fits one of the key driving factors: collaboration. Open-source code is developed by several people (even thousands) working together to make a usable tool or program. Even when it's finished, some of these same people (or others) can and will continue to improve on it for the goodness of all. Using open-source code can help you develop programs, tools, and even Web sites that can be used in your marketing efforts.

Behind every software program you use (for example, Microsoft Office), there is code that tells it how to function and behave. For proprietary reasons, this code is typically patented, copyrighted, trademarked, and locked up tight so that unauthorized people can't mess around with it. Developers, and the businesses for which those developers are working, don't want someone ripping off their code or taking the code and then making a similar program.

Many programmers and businesses have decided that it is in the common good to write code and then make it available to the public to improve on. I love the analogy of comparing open-source code to a potluck picnic. Everyone gets to bring something and, from the various individual contributions, a full meal is made. The concept is essentially the same. With open-source code, the meat is typically provided by another programmer, and then others are invited to add to it and make it a full, working program that people would want to use. The best part: It's free. As with a potluck, because you brought something with you, there is no cost to you.

With collaboration being the model of choice for many people, open-source code has thrown the software model on its head. The code that's behind the software tool you are running would be visible and free for use. This would be like Microsoft saying, "Hey, we know you love Microsoft Outlook, so here's the code; use the program and code for free. In fact, feel free to improve on it, make it better, and, while you're at it, sell your new software for a profit."

Using Open-Source Code

Open-source code is gaining so much popularity for many reasons:

- Software sales are drastically down. Consumers and businesses are looking to the Web for more Web-based solutions rather than buying CDs and programs that will need to be updated often.

- Using open-source code can save you money. As this book is being written, the U.S. unemployment rate is nearly 10%, and we're in one of the worst recessions we have seen in decades. Using open-source code can be very cost-effective.

- Open-source code offers the benefit of a wide diversity of collaborators who are working independently, often throughout the world, unburdened by corporate politics. The spirit of volunteerism and independent creativity fosters maverick innovation that can often lead to a stronger, more useful product.

- Collaboration is the new model. As you will learn in the next chapter, collaboration is critical for success. You cannot live in a box thinking you know everything!

There are, however, a few key disadvantages to open-source code:

- It can be costly to maintain the platform for others to collaborate on. Someone needs to maintain the server, the bandwidth, and the technology that others are collaborating on. Because open-source code is typically given away, you could be spending money and going through a lot of trouble without directly benefiting from the results.

- Quality control is nonexistent. Although it is great to have many people contributing their coding and creativity, their skill levels may not be up to the quality you might expect from the big-name companies.

- As with cooking, everyone has their own style of coding. This, in my opinion, is the biggest downfall to open-source code. One person's coding style can be drastically different from the way another codes. You end up getting a final product that may have all different types of code when it could have been a bit simpler.

- You would get minimal support, if any.

To Do

How to Leverage Open-Source Code:

In this case, we're talking only about how to use others' code for your business or personal use, rather than from a programming standpoint of collaborating on the code while it's in development.

Step 1: *Find what you're looking for.*

What type of software are you looking for? Chances are that whatever you are looking for has some type of open-source code software out there. Go to www.Google.com and type in *Open Source* and then whatever software you're looking for—for example, *open source content-management system.*

Step 1.5: *See whether there is some raw code instead of an out-of-the-box solution.*

Here are some sites to get the code from:

- www.Koders.com

- www.SourceForge.net

- www.CodeBeach.com

- www.Planet-Source-Code.com

Step 2: *Evaluate the open-source programs out there before selecting one.*

As with physical software, there are typically many alternatives that accomplish the same thing. Do your research, and read the message boards, forums, and so on to choose the best software to manipulate.

Step 3: *Get it going.*

Start using the software as is or hire a programmer to manipulate the code. Typically you are going to want to hire a programmer to help with the coding aspect to make the software even better and to suit your needs.

Also bear in mind that many open-source programs can be used with no manipulation.

Here are some of my current favorite open-source software tools:

- **Firefox:** The browser of choice for most.

- **OpenOffice.org:** Don't want to give Microsoft any more money? Leverage OpenOffice.org and their suite of tools.

- **Joomla:** Among the best content-management systems available today.

- **Drupal:** This is another content-management system. Many programmers have been using Drupal to configure their entire Web sites and shopping carts.

- **WordPress:** This is the blogging platform of choice. We have developed more than 15,000 WordPress blogs and sites to date. We are also using a software tool called WishList Member to design WordPress member sites. There are hundreds of people all over the world constantly working on and making WordPress better and better.

- **PortableApps:** Plain and simple, this tool aims to make all your apps portable on a USB drive. You can carry all your favorite programs on a small device and use them on any computer!

- **MediaWiki:** Originally developed by Wikipedia, it allows for easy collaboration.

Step 4: *Make available the code adjustments you hired the programmer to make.*

Because the open-source movement is all about collaboration, why not give back? Post the coding adjustments (as long as they are not proprietary) to the open-source community so that others can build on the changes you had made.

Tas Tip

If you drastically improve an open-source-code software tool and pay a programmer considerable money to do so, you will want to look at rebranding and selling it. Before doing so, learn about the rules and regulations of the open-source code you are using. This is a great way to make some extra money and pay for your development costs!

That's it. Using open-source code is actually quite easy. With the growing number of people looking to use open-source code rather than purchasing traditional software, chances are you will find some type of open-source software tool already out there in cyberspace to leverage and/or improve on your needs!

9

Collaboration: Connecting and Sharing Data at Lightning-Speed Paces

Everyone wants things quicker than the day before. Taz Solutions, Inc., is actually the fourth company I have started and grown. After experiencing issues in the other three, I knew that I had to learn everything I could about different systems that could help a business run more effectively. After much research and chats with different people using these various systems, I realized that Web-based systems were the way to go. I came to this conclusion from two paths: The first was that I found from speaking with others that it's much cheaper in the long run to use Web-based systems. The second was that I wanted to hire and work with people throughout the world. I wasn't going to maintain some massive server in my home office for everyone. I'd rather have the systems I purchased cover that cost.

This chapter is to help you improve (or establish) your Web 3.0 marketing systems.

Collaboration is critical for success in today's marketplace. There are many businesses that are being run by one person, but chances are that even that one person has a team of vendors or contractors who are helping with business functions such as marketing, fulfillment, accounting, and general administrative support. Even the Fortune 500 companies use independent contractors or consultants and, more often than not, the contractors work off the business's premises. This poses a data-sharing issue as well as a potential delay in getting and sharing the information. With Web 3.0, every day—every hour—counts in terms of your competitiveness and performance.

Web-based applications can help you effectively manage all of your team members (internal and external), as well as increase your speed to market.

There are hundreds of ways teams can collaborate, but I've zeroed in on the most important, the ones that will make the biggest difference to your speed and competitive edge:

- Chatting
- Sharing docs, files, audios, videos
- Project management
- Analytics
- Shopping-cart system
- E-mail management
- Customer relationship management
- Teleconferences/webinars

Keep in mind that the software tools I will be recommending have been or are being used by my companies or our clients. I will never recommend something I cannot deem as useful, affordable, and a tool you will see a solid ROI from. Since there are more than 15 tools I'm recommending, I'm not going to give you a traditional how-to, step-by-step, as I have previously. Rather, I'm providing some specifics you should be aware of.

Google Apps

Google Apps is a collection of tools designed and hosted by Google. Google Apps started off with Google Mail and has expanded drastically from there. For $50 a year (at this writing), you get the following:

- E-mail accounts
- Calendars
- Google Docs (docs, spreadsheets, forms, and presentations)
- Chatting capabilities (voice and text)
- Mini portal sites
- Contact management
- Customizable home page (iGoogle)
- Translation
- Picasa (photo sharing)
- And much more (check out www.google.com/apps)

To Do

How to Implement Google Apps into Your Company:

Step 1: *Sign up.*

Go to www.google.com/a and sign up for Google Apps.

Step 2: *Verify.*

Follow the technical details on how to verify your domain name. Typically, it simply means posting a page on your site to prove you have ownership.

Step 3: *Configure.*

Configure your e-mail. This will involve changing your MX records wherever your Web site is hosted. This tells your hosting company that Google is now hosting your e-mail. Your e-mail will be *example@yourdomain.com*.

Step 4: *Create.*

Create your different user accounts for all your employees and "virtual employees." Keep in mind that there is a small fee, so don't get crazy, but also don't skimp!

Step 5: *Personalize.*

Set up your e-mail settings, under the Settings tab, when logged in to Google Apps.

- Set up a signature.

- Link it with Microsoft Outlook or other mail clients, if applicable.

- Set up filters. Instead of using traditional folders, Google Mail uses something called filters. This allows you to direct any mail that comes from janedoe@janedoe.com to a filter called Jane Doe.

- Color-code things to your liking for easier access.

Step 6: *Schedule.*

After you have your e-mail set up, move to your calendar. If you're a Microsoft Exchange user, this will save you money. Have your employees use their Google calendars and share accordingly. Depending on your structure, some people should be able to help manage your calendar, with others having only viewing privileges. This, too, can sync with your BlackBerry and Microsoft Outlook.

Step 7: *Centralize.*

Get everyone using Google Docs. I love the mail and calendar apps, but I adore Google Docs! Here, you can create, edit, and manage the following:

- Documents (like Microsoft Word documents).

- Spreadsheets (like Microsoft Excel documents).

- Presentations (like Microsoft PowerPoint documents).

- Forms. Any type of paper document that you need someone to fill out can be designed in here and submitted virtually!

What is awesome about Google Docs is that multiple people can be viewing a document, form, spreadsheet, or presentation at the same time and making changes with each other live. This solves the issue of some people not having the most up-to-date version of a particular document.

These are some uses (there are thousands):

- Collaborating on your marketing calendar
- Pulling in analytical reports
- Sharing company documents, like your handbook and policies
- Keeping track of usernames and passwords with spreadsheets
- Managing personal or business finances
- Keeping résumés in one place
- Requesting vacation time off, using a Google form

Make sure that, after creating the file, you click on the Share Files link. Invite people who will view the document and those who should be able to make changes to it.

Step 8: *Link.*

Set up mini portal sites. You can set up unlimited mini portal sites and share them with the appropriate persons. We have used these for managing different projects. These portal sites then allow you to link to the various other Google Apps.

Case Study

We recently launched a new version of our Web site. As you are well aware, there are many moving parts to a Web site launch. Because we are Google Apps fanatics, we launched a mini portal site devoted to the redesign of our Web site. We invited the seven people who were involved in the design process.

On the portal site, we had the following:

- A calendar that everyone could see and manage with all the critical dates, meetings, and deadlines.

- Google forms to be filled out daily, reporting on progress.

- A Microsoft Excel file with all the links to the different pages that would be on the site.

- A presentation on the vision of the site that everyone could come back and watch to make sure that the build out was in line with the blueprint.

- Fifty-plus Google documents with all the new Web site content, shared with our copywriters.

- A countdown tool showing how many days we had left until the launch date.

It was wonderful to have one central place to have all of this information to collaborate.

The Takeaways:

- This tool saved us time and money from having to conduct dozens of unnecessary phone calls and long e-mail exchanges.

- Everything was virtual, so we could access it from anywhere (including from my BlackBerry on the beach)!

- We launched the site three weeks ahead of schedule.

Step 9: *Leverage.*

Leverage some of the many other Google Apps:

- Mobile: Get your apps right on your phone.

- Google short URLs (like www.tinyurl.com). Make the URL much easier to remember.

- Google Web sites: Publish simple Web sites with ease.

- Contacts: A great contact-management system to keep your contacts information stored and updated virtually.

Step 10: *Follow up.*

Collaboration is only as good as the collaborators using the tools available to them. So make sure your team is using their collaboration tools to their fullest extent. You can't have some people sending docs through e-mail, others through Google Docs, some on Google's mail system, and others on something else. Your goal is 100% adoption.

Tas Tip

Without full user adoption implementing new systems will not be of service to you. Understand that in the beginning, adoption may take some time to get everyone fully utilizing the new tools and systems, but in the long run, everyone has got to be on the same page.

How You Can Leverage Collaboration Tools

Collaboration Tool 1: Chatting

You need to be able to communicate with your team quickly and effectively. With the costs of travel rising, chatting with video has become more popular. Rather than purchasing expensive hardware, leverage one of the many free or low-cost tools. Most newer computers already have built-in functionality to make chatting much easier than before.

Picking one tool and using it exclusively is a much better strategy than using various chatting platforms. I also recommend using video whenever possible. Since I have a large virtual company and rarely see people face to face more than once a year, it's nice to see their smiling faces on webcam from time to time!

Tools to Use:

- **Gmail chat:** You can chat with text, audio, and now also video.

- **www.Skype.com:** We replaced our VOIP-phone systems with Skype for a $18,000 annual savings. All of our employees, contractors, and vendors are required to use Skype to chat with us. We use text chat for quick questions, voice for conference calls and meetings, and video when conducting one-on-one meetings. We also have started using one of Skype's newest features, screen sharing, making it an even greater all-in-one solution. This allows you to view someone else's desktop in real time. Watch out, www.WebEx.com and www.GoToMeeting.com!

- **www.ooVoo.com:** This application allows you to chat over the Web with text, voice, and video. The advantage of ooVoo is that you can see multiple people's webcams as opposed to only one.

Collaboration Tool 2: Sharing Docs, Audios, Videos, and Files

Because the chances of you and everyone else being on the same network are slim to none, you need to have a central place and Web systems in place to share and work on together with ease.

Digital storage and file sharing is critical. You need to keep backups on hard drives, as well as in digital locations. With file sharing, it's great to be able to work with your team on documents at the same time and see who has accessed and downloaded certain files.

Tools to Use:

- **Google Apps:** You can share and work on documents, spreadsheets, and presentations all in one place.

- **www.Box.net:** I use this tool for two things. First, I have an account where I back up my hard drive daily. Second, we have a company account. If clients want to send us large files (like audio or video), we ask them to upload the files to Box.net and then share them with us. There is a free version of Box.net as well as a paid one allowing you more storage and faster uploads.

Collaboration Tool 3: Project Management

There are a lot of moving pieces to Web site design, marketing, product creation, and beyond. Tracking all the different pieces can be a nightmare because there are typically different people working on different parts at different times. More important, there are always different things that need to be finished before you can move onto something else. This is like the game Jenga. If you pull out pieces here and there, the whole tower will come crashing down. Much as with chatting collaboration, you can't leverage multiple project-management tools. It doesn't make sense to have different pieces in different locations.

Tools to Use:

- **Google Apps and Sites:** The earlier case study details how we used Google Sites to manage the launch of our new and improved Web site. It's very easy to use. The only drawback is the inability to set clear tasks with follow-up actions.

- **Basecamp:** You can find this product at the Web site www.37signals.com. It is a project-management system that is very boiled down and easy to use. We use it in our organization to track all of our design projects.

- **www.AtTask.com:** Similar in nature to Basecamp, AtTask allows you to manage multiple projects, tasks, and workflow modules. The tool is relatively straightforward and is also being used by a lot of top companies.

Collaboration Tool 4: Analytics

What you don't track, you can't measure. If you don't know where your traffic is coming from, you are losing out on very valuable data that will allow you to make strategic decisions much more quickly.

With analytics, you need to track everything as thoroughly as possible. Every page on your Web site should have a tracking code installed, and each and every promotion you do should have the capability to be tracked. For example, if you are running a mobile-marketing campaign, set up a unique landing page and install analytics on that page. Use that landing page for only that promotion to get the most accurate information.

Tools to Use:

- **Google Analytics:** This tool will blow your mind when you adopt it! There are 250-page books written on how to use Google Analytics to improve your decision-making abilities by tracking everything related to your Web site.

- **Google Webmaster Tools:** This allows you to really see how Google views and crawls/indexes your Web site. It also allows you to diagnose various site problems, learn more about the different links coming to and from your site, and even add a sitemap.

To Do

How to Use Google Analytics:

Step 1: *Install.*

Install the tracking code on your site. Make sure that the code is installed on every page on your site.

Step 2: *Wait.*

Wait a solid seven days before starting to look at trends. It takes some time for the data to start pulling.

Step 3: *Implement.*

Use the various tools to analyze and understand the data:

- **Unique Visitors:** This is the number of people who visit your site, excluding duplicates. For instance, if someone visits your site 100 times in the same day, it will not be counted more than once.

- **Page Views:** Page views represent the number of total pages viewed across your site. For instance, say you have ten visitors and 100 page views. This would mean that, among those ten people, 100 pages across your site were viewed, with an average of ten page views per visitor.

- **Bounce Rate:** This is the percentage of people who visit only one page, or exit on the page they came into. We typically consider the bounce rate as people who are not interested in what we have to offer because they didn't explore other pages the site offers.

- **Average Time on Site:** Care to know how long the average person stays on your site? This will give you that data!

- **New vs. Returning:** Seeing how many people are new to your site for the first time gives you some great information. I use this to make sure that I'm attracting new people, as well as returning visitors to my blog to read the content.

- **Traffic Sources:** This is, in my opinion, the most critical area to analyze. Traffic sources show you all the places you're getting Web traffic from. This will confirm whether the marketing tactics you're using are actually driving traffic. For example, if you spent five hours on Ustream.TV, did that actually produce some traffic?

Step 4: *Enhance your understanding of who your visitors are and what they want.*

More advanced tools will give you even deeper understanding of the people who are coming to your site:

- **Site Overlay:** This tool will show you the different places where people are clicking or taking action on your site. This data has caused us to do multiple redesigns to many sites. You can quickly see whether people are clicking on your opt-in, for example, or a different part of your site. If they are not taking the actions you are hoping they take, see where they are clicking and move your site around to accommodate.

- **Map Overlay:** This will show you all the different countries people are from who are visiting your site.

- **Content:** It's very powerful to see what pages attract visitors and where they typically exit. With this knowledge, you will see whether you need to beef up the content to keep your visitors longer— or entice them to return.

- **IP Banning:** To get an ever better estimate of your traffic, you can tell Google Analytics which computers to not include in your statistics (typically yours and your Web team's).

- **Goals:** Put in your conversion goals and track your progress of the number of people who purchase.

- **Event Tracking:** Track all the different traffic for a particular time-sensitive promotion.

- **Custom Reporting:** Design a report that makes the most sense for your business—for example, unique visitors week over week.

- **Browser Capability:** This will show which browsers, operating systems, and screen sizes are being used to view your site. If you know your site doesn't work well with Macs, yet 20% of your visitors are Mac users, you have some adjustments to make!

Step 5: *Make changes.*

Make changes to your Web site and your marketing in relation to the data. You will quickly be able to see which marketing strategy is working.

Case Study

Discount Tire provides people with various options and pricing for tires and wheels, either at retail locations or for purchase on the Internet. Discount Tire is the largest independent tire dealer in the nation, with 600 stores selling only tires and wheels.

Discount Tire implemented Google Analytics across its sites. Although many of the departments leveraged and made great use of this data, I'd like to focus on their marketing department in this example. The marketing department stated using the summary screens at their executive meetings. The data showed simple conclusions: the return on investment based on the data was overwhelming. This led the management team to allocate much more funds to Web marketing.

The Result: Discount Tire increased sales 14% the first week by using Google Analytics.

Collaboration Tool 5: Shopping Cart

How can you take orders without a shopping-cart system? Go with something that is Web-based so that you constantly have the latest and greatest version without paying for costly upgrades. If you have some complex customizations, you will need to take this fact into consideration. Many of the Web-based-only solutions will not be able to accommodate hundreds of custom fields.

Tools to Use:

- **www.Amazingshoppingcart.com:** An all-in-one solution like this is the best route to take. With www.Amazingshoppingcart.com, your cart, e-mail database, and affiliates are all managed through its portal.

- **www.ClickBank.com:** It is one of the leaders in making digital-product selling and delivery a breeze. What rocks about ClickBank is that it handles the payment gateway, delivery, and the service end for you. You will pay a premium for this service, but it will save you money in the long run because you won't have to pay for an accountant to handle payments or a customer service representative. ClickBank will also handle your affiliates and cut them checks directly!

- **www.Infusionsoft.com:** Infusionsoft is an all-in-one solution similar to www.Amazingshoppingcart.com.

I recommend that if you're starting out, you start with www.Amazingshoppingcart.com. If you are already generating sales, Infusionsoft is a great tool to evaluate. It is a great solution for e-commerce businesses because it also has customer-relationship-management features built in.

Collaboration Tool 6: E-Mail Marketing

We live in an e-mail-driven world. E-mail is among the simplest ways to get content to people quickly.

Keep your e-mails simple, short, to the point, filled with great content and a solid, clear call to action. Understanding that many people will be reading your e-mails on a mobile device is the key here. You don't want to clutter up your e-mails with designs, forms, templates, and logos.

Lastly, it's all about the e-mail subject. Because everyone is busier than ever, they also scan and delete e-mails quickly. If your subject is not compelling, forget it! Spend 75% of your time working on the e-mail subject and 25% on the content in the actual e-mail.

Tools to Use:

- **www.Amazingshoppingcart.com:** If you take our advice and leverage this all-in-one solution, your e-mail marketing is included, allowing you to send full-blown HTML e-mails and templates along with tracking features.

Tas Tip

Get yourself on a dedicated IP with www.Amazingshoppingcart.com to drastically increase your deliverability rate! This allows your e-mail blasts to come from a server other than everyone else's. So you don't get "penalized" when others send spam e-mails.

- **www.AWeber.com:** This is considered the gold standard by many Internet marketers. Its system is easy to use and has great results.

- **www.iContact.com:** It is a solid company that really understands e-mail marketing. What I really like about iContact is that they also train you about the ins and outs of e-mail marketing (education-based marketing).

- **www.VerticalResponse.com:** If you're using Salesforce.com and need to blast your entire database, this is the tool to use. They also have a standalone solution, but I much prefer the solutions mentioned previously over VerticalResponse.

- **www.Infusionsoft.com:** Many firms are making a switch over their solution because of the advanced e-mail segmenting. You can drill down to very specific details to provide for a much more targeted e-mail campaign.

Case Study

Big Peach Running Company is an Atlanta-based retailer that specializes in footwear, apparel, and accessories for the community's runners and walkers. The company differentiates itself from other impersonal large sporting-goods stores and mall-based locations by catering to those participating in a "pedestrian active lifestyle." They focus on providing the proper footwear fitted to the individual's needs based on biomechanics, foot characteristics, fit, feel, and ride.

Big Peach uses newsletters to reach out and inform the community on events, races, walks, and clinics. The problem facing Big Peach was that whenever they launched a newsletter, their Web site's hosting company's server would get locked up for five to six hours at a time. Their database of 35,000 people was just too large.

The solution was iContact, which allowed Big Peach to easily create permission-based e-mail newsletters for their large community of runners and walkers.

The Results:

- Big Peach now is able to keep track of newsletter stats, such as the number of people opening the newsletters, resulting in more effective marketing.

- The cost of the iContact fee is less than their original Web host company's fee, so Big Peach is saving money while improving their community outreach.

- Although Big Peach does not directly sell products through their newsletter, they are seeing incremental sales increases by utilizing this informative tool. By informing the community, they are gaining interest in their product.

Collaboration Tool 7: Customer Relationship Management

Customer relationship management, or CRM, is one of the fastest-growing customer-service trends today. Because it is becoming increasingly difficult to acquire new customers, you'd better make sure you are servicing your current ones and tending to any fresh leads appropriately!

Use the tool to manage leads, opportunities, customers, and other important company information. The key to successful customer relationship management is having all the necessary data, files, and activity in a central place. For example, Matthew Ferry International uses Salesforce.com to track the different events its customers have attended and what products they have purchased, along with hundreds of other lines of information like address, birthday, spouse's name, and beyond. They use this information to help their sales team close more businesses and to effectively stay in touch with their clients and prospects. It's become their main command center for the business.

Here are a few insights into choosing a CRM solution that best fits you and your business:

- Whichever tool you use, make sure that it is Web-based.
- One hundred percent user adoption is critical. Anyone who has a touch point with a prospect or customer has to be using the tool and entering data on a regular basis. If one person in a department doesn't adopt the solution, you're going to be missing out on valuable data and will not have a full view of all customer activity.

Tools to Use:
- www.Salesforce.com
- www.Infusionsoft.com
- www.SugarCRM.com

In this case, I'm featuring Salesforce.com because it's the tool we use along with the vast majority of our clients. I encourage you to check out all the different CRM solutions before making a decision on the one you want to use.

What really surprises me is the fact that very few businesses actually use any type of CRM solution. Many businesses track leads and customers in Outlook, Excel, Word, or even on paper. These tools are not meant for customer management. You really need to have a solid CRM solution to help you grow your business or you're going to have data all over the place and the need to play catch-up when your business takes off. I'm a big proponent of putting systems in place that are scalable.

Salesforce.com is a total CRM solution. It is the leader in this space and has been, in my opinion, from Day One. The big difference between Salesforce.com and many of the other CRM solutions is that it is 100% Web-based. This means that there is absolutely no software to purchase, and you can be up and running in minutes. The other big advantage is the cost savings in going with a Web-based solution. Your IT management costs with Salesforce.com are very minimal because it's all maintained by Salesforce.com. Rather, if you're using a software-based product, your IT department is going to have to maintain the software on its servers, and you're going to have additional hard costs related to that software.

My favorite thing about CRM and Salesforce.com, in particular, is that everything can be housed in one place: all your leads, customers, contracts, documents, employee information, financial information, and beyond. If you add in all the different apps in the app exchange, there is a limitless amount of potential for all the different things you can do. I've known clients and customers who use Salesforce.com to essentially run their entire business. As I mentioned previously, between this tool and Google Apps, we pretty much run our entire virtual company.

To Do

How to Use Salesforce.com:

Step 1: *Sign up.*

Go to www.Salesforce.com and sign up for the professional version. There are other versions, but the professional or enterprise editions are the way to go. Currently, the professional edition is $65 per user per month.

Step 2: *Make a list.*

Make a list of all the different in-house activities that you want to use and track in Salesforce.com—for example, your leads, contracts, employees, e-mails, and pipeline. This becomes your wish list. Keep things priori-tized, and star the items that are critical. Put the starred items at the top of the list so that you will work your way down your priorities at the next step.

Step 3: *Customize.*

Using this list, you can see all the customizations you will need to make in order for the solution to fit your company.

Keep in mind that you can even start using Salesforce.com right out of the box. If you're a smaller company, I recommend you start using Salesforce.com as is before doing a lot of massive upgrades.

Step 4: *Specialize.*

If you require a lot of additional customization, hire a certified Salesforce.com specialist. Various people know Salesforce.com well. You want someone who not only is a very good programmer, but also understands processes and business flow so that they can make sure your solution suits your current needs and anticipates what additional changes you may have as you grow.

Step 5: *Train.*

Train your users on how to use the system.

Step 6: *Adopt.*

For any CRM solution to be effective, you must have 100% adoption.

Step 7: *Add apps.*

As your business continues to expand, consider adding different apps to your solution. Visit Salesforce.com to see all the apps they have available. Install an app or two at a time, train your users on how to use the new app, and make sure that it fits your business.

Some of my favorite apps include the following:

- **Google Integration:** This allows for documents to be linked in Salesforce.com along with outbound and inbound e-mails.

- **VerticalResponse:** This is a tool for e-mail marketing. It allows you to send highly customized e-mails that are also tracked in Salesforce.com. When looking at your contacts, you can segment out who viewed, deleted, opened, and clicked on the e-mail.

- **Genius:** This app tracks open rates of e-mails to see how many people are reading them. With Genius, you have a little box up on your computer screen. The box tells you if anyone is viewing your e-mail live.

- **Hoover's:** This gives us the competitive intelligence we're looking for. Hoover's provides information as to the size of the company, key decision makers, recent news, and beyond. I like to be armed with as much information as possible before talking to a prospect.

How we use Salesforce.com:

- Every lead, referral, and prospect is entered and tracked here.

- After we determine that a lead has revenue potential, we convert it into an opportunity. We forecast based on opportunities: expected close date, expected close percentage, and the dollar value.

- All customers and data are housed in Salesforce.com. Every e-mail and greeting card sent, every phone call placed, and other activities are entered here. Anything that relates to our customers is tracked.

- All employees are tracked in Salesforce.com, including contracts, pictures, personal information, wages, job description, and the like.

- Our live events are managed with the event plug-in designed by Salesforce.com.

Case Study

Segway sells a product that allows you to get around more efficiently while staying green. I'm sure you have seen a tour guide on a Segway, people cruising around New York City, or even police officers using the devices.

Segway's original challenge was to find a solution that integrated all the various individuals and businesses that would need information throughout the world. They also wanted to bring sales and marketing together. So they decided to roll out a Salesforce.com integration. Their integration included materials and tools for sales, marketing, and a partner management system.

The Results:

- Their dealers, partners, and corporate users now have all the information they need at their fingertips.

- On the sales front, the sales team has the visibility it was missing; it can finally see the entire sales channel to increase sales.

- Marketing finally is able to understand what people want by having much better insight. They are able to see which marketing dollars are actually working. In addition, their marketing reps now approve sales leads and assign them to the best dealer possible. The entire process from start to finish can now be tracked!

Collaboration Tool 8: Teleconferences and Webinars

We use teleconferences and webinars to collaborate with each other, our prospects, and our clients. In terms of effectiveness when trying to close business, we prefer to use a webinar because it allows us to give visuals, making things easier to understand. When we're delivering presentations to the masses, we tend to just use audio and conduct these in the evening, when most people will have finished eating. We use audio for these larger groups because a lot of people will be multitasking or listening on a mobile phone while driving. If we need to make a key point using visuals, those people are going to miss the boat completely.

Tools to Use:

- **www.GoToWebinar.com:** GoToWebinar allows you to have a phone bridge of up to 1,000 people and share your screen or presentation. We use this tool when we're conducting educational presentations to both prospects and our virtual team.

- **Adobe Connect:** This tool has a very clean-cut platform that's easy to use. Adobe Connect is starting to pick up some steam in the Web-conferencing arena.

- **www.WebEx.com:** This tool is Cisco's product. It competes directly with GoToMeeting and GoToWebinar.

- **www.Dimdim.com:** Why pay for Web conferencing? www.Dimdim.com is 100% free.

- **www.FreeConferencing.com:** A 1,000-line phone bridge for free! I'm sure this will change, but it will be very low cost. I use this tool almost daily.

- **www.ooVoo.com:** This tool allows you to host a conference call and see multiple webcams at the same time. We use it to chat with our customers as well as prospects.

On-Demand/Software as a Service

Now that you know all the different tools that you can use to speed up your marketing and communication across the board, your next opportunity is to figure out how to put all this information to your strategic benefit.

If you review all the tools we recommend, there is only one that is not Web-based (Microsoft Office Suite). This didn't happen by accident. We prefer things that are Web-based and available on demand. The mantra in the technology world is *software as a service* (SaaS). This simply means that the provider licenses you the tool to use as a service on demand.

The reason it's being mentioned in this Web 3.0 book is that most companies are still not up to speed on leveraging software as a service platform and Web-based tools to speed up their marketing and collaboration. Many of them are still using clunky systems. Remember the example I talked about in the CRM system about companies using Microsoft Excel to track leads? I love the program, but come on now, you need to get up to speed as quickly as possible because the trends are changing quickly.

Here are the key driving factors:

- Reducing costs (original purchase, IT costs, and lifetime cost of ownership)
- Speed to implementation
- More companies going virtual
- Can be used from anywhere in the world
- Allows for easier collaboration
- Many add-ons that can go along with the solution

Some limitations of the SaaS model are listed here:

- If you can't access the Internet, you won't have access to these services unless an offline version is available.

- Different Internet access speeds could be frustrating when you're working in a team with members all over the country.

- There are security risks. If someone obtains your login/password, he or she may be able to access the information you're able to see. That person will also need to be on your computer or get access to your e-mail to verify before logging in, so there are extra measures in place before anyone can fully breach your account.

- Extensive customizations can get expensive.

Out of all of these benefits and limitations, reducing costs gets the most attention. Your IT costs dramatically decrease when you're using software as a service. Some examples include the following:

- ACT versus Web-based CRM, like www.Salesforce.com

- In-house phone system versus www.Skype.com

- Shopping cart software versus www.Amazingshoppingcart.com

Use the software-as-a-service model to gain speed in your marketing and collaboration with employees, vendors, prospects, and clients. Now is the time to start switching over your systems and planning for the future. The best part: Even if you use only a few of the tools we mentioned, you're going to see an immediate return on your investment. That investment may come in the form of saving you time, money, or energy. Collaboration and the desire for the most up-to-date services to be delivered more quickly will keep this fire fueled for many years to come. My recommendation: Make the switches and don't look back. Trust me, you will be glad you did!

10

Web 3.0 Companies

This chapter is about companies that I consider to be game changers and in a whole different league from the rest. While analyzing Web 3.0 companies, I analyzed more than 100 enterprises across various sectors. I noticed that several shared similar qualities:

- Have unique traits and habits
- Started small and grew rapidly
- Are considered or becoming a household name
- Are using the Web 3.0 marketing tactics profiled
- Are pioneers in their space

Yes, there were other factors I noticed, such as growth rates, employee satisfaction, and size, but these less-tangible qualities were the ones that stuck out to me the most. Armed with a whole slew of intangible information, I have selected four companies that I deem to be innovators and companies exhibiting Web 3.0 business and marketing tactics.

One thing I want to point out is that many small companies are leveraging some of the Web 3.0 marketing tactics I've presented in the book. However, I have yet to find a company (besides my own) that is leveraging *all the tactics* I've presented. The four companies profiled here are leveraging all the *tools*. Don't be discouraged if you're a smaller business—it's not just large companies who can use Web 3.0 marketing. As I've shown throughout the book, any company, regardless of size, can deploy these methods.

The four companies I selected are Amazon, Zappos, Salesforce.com, and Cisco. Check out their profiles to see why I consider them Web 3.0 companies. These four companies are no exception!

Company: Amazon

Web site: www.Amazon.com

When you think of Amazon, you might think books. Granted, Amazon did start off by selling books, but it soon starting selling pretty much anything you would desire, from CDs to deodorant to kitchen knives and everything in between.

Amazon has the distinction of being America's largest online retailer. Try to top that one, Wal-Mart! It puts the customer first in all respects. Amazon tracks your browsing and buying trends. Armed with that information, it creates a unique customer experience tailored to you! When was the last time you logged on to your favorite Web site and the home page was different each time and, oddly enough, packed with only things you might be interested in?

Keeping the customers first has drastically fueled its growth. What's great about this company is that it is run by innovators who are constantly trying new ways to improve the customer's experience. They recently launched Amazon S3, included a section for self-publishing books, promoted their famous Kindle device, and even purchased Zappos. I'd say they have diversified themselves quite well as leaders!

Why It's a Web 3.0 Company

Business side:

- **Kindle:** This is Amazon's wireless reading device that allows you to read eBooks on the go as if you were reading an actual book (eliminating eye strain). You can find, buy, and read books instantly with its wireless access. You don't need Internet access to do this.

- **Amazon S3:** This is a highly scalable storage solution based on their proprietary technology.

- **One-click ordering:** I have a love-hate relationship with this. I think it's awesome that with one click of the mouse, I just ordered a product. The downside: It causes me to buy without thinking. Just visiting Amazon now caused me to preorder the next season of *The Office*.

- **User-customized experience:** This is what makes the company among my favorites! When you log in to Amazon, your screen is tailored to your personal buying and browsing habits. Don't like something they are showing you? Take it off instantly!

- **Self-publishing books:** Need to self-publish? Use Amazon's platform to get a book out into the universe!

- **Innovation:** It comes from the bottom. I told you they are innovators, but what Amazon really understands is that innovation doesn't simply come from the top!

Marketing side:

- **Amazon reviews:** This feature encourages user interaction in rating and writing reviews for different products. Amazon was among the first to offer reviews, and since then, reviews have become the norm on e-commerce-based sites.

- **Testing:** Its technology team is constantly tweaking and making things better.

- **Mobile site:** In addition to www.Amazon.com, the company operates a site that can be better viewed from a cellphone browser than can the regular site (a subsidiary of Amazon also owns a mobile marketing firm).

- **Virtual reality worlds:** Amazon has a presence on Second Life and many other VR worlds.

Company: Zappos

Web site: www.Zappos.com

Zappos is an e-commerce site that focuses on shoes, but it has many additional product offerings, from clothing and bags to accessories and sunglasses. It has gained a lot of forward momentum and awareness recently after the company went from zero to $1 billion in sales in nine years. Not only are people and businesses talking about its sales, but they also are really excited about the company's culture and service. Zappos prides itself on its unique culture and its commitment and dedication to customer service. The company loves doing things that are not considered the norm. For example, there is free shipping, a 365-day return policy, and 24/7 customer service. Furthermore, if they don't have a product in stock, the call-center agent will locate the product on a competitor's site for you!

On a final note, the buzzword around Zappos is happiness! Their vision is delivering happiness to customers, employees, and vendors.

Why It's a Web 3.0 Company

Business side:

- This company is constantly on the leading edge in their marketplace.

- They do things differently! Reread their vision state-ment. I have never read a vision like that before.
- They aren't afraid to spend money to test things out or on training.
- Customer-service reps are rewarded for spending *more* time on the phone with customers.
- They encourage individuality.

Marketing side:

- At Zappos, testing is the name of the game. They have tested pretty much any and every type of marketing form on the planet to see what works and what doesn't.
- They have had such great marketing success that they have a subscription service, Zappos Insights, that allows you to learn more from them.
- Twitter is being leveraged constantly. They have a mas-sive Twitter following, and employees are encouraged to use Twitter to communicate. Not only do they use it, but they treat their Twitter followers like raving fans and give many Twitter-only specials.
- They use open-source technology rather than propri-etary technology to save on IT costs.
- They are rolling out a www.Zappos.com mobile site.
- They maintain an internal Wiki for employees to col-laborate on.
- They have developed various mobile Web apps.
- They track *everything*.

Company: Salesforce.com

Web site: www.Salesforce.com

You already know about Salesforce.com because we discussed it in the chapter on collaboration. The company prides itself on two things: applications for customer-relationship management and their Force.com platform. In my opinion, they have also defined and shaped the software as a service industry.

They are best known for their Web-based CRM system that allows you to track and manage prospects, customers, employees, contracts, and beyond. Essentially anything that relates to your company can be stored and developed in Salesforce.com. We use it to manage all of our leads and customers. Using their AppExchange, we have continued to deck out our Salesforce.com experience to make it further suit our business.

Switching gears, they recently released Force.com. Force.com is among the easiest places to build out business applications and even Web sites. It's a simplified programming model in a cloud-based environment. For marketers, this may not mean much. Rephrased in English for the rest of us, it's a place to build open-source types of programs to be leveraged.

Why It's a Web 3.0 Company

Business side:

- Salesforce.com is constantly on the leading edge in the technology marketplace. Attend one of their Dreamforce conferences, and you will be even further blown out of your seat as to where this company is headed! They always announce the latest and greatest changes to the platform, allow for on-the-spot customization, and host various breakout sessions to help you use their tool. This information is only the tip of the iceberg.

- They understand that the growing model is Web-based, and they view software as a service.

- Collaboration is king. Their users can collaborate with one another, across companies, with the Salesforce.com team of employees, programmers, and developers alike. There is very little closed communication across the company. Free-flowing information and ideas have helped keep this company growing strong.

- The AppExchange has thousands of applications that others have developed for use with their platform.

- They allow developers to run free. They call it enterprise cloud computing. It's built on their Force.com platform. Build an application and share it with the world!

- Salesforce.com can be run on virtually any device. They understood far sooner than most that things were changing.

Marketing side:

- They have been leveraging all the marketing tactics we've talked about in the book, many of them for years. Need I say more?

Company: Cisco

Web site: www.cisco.com

Founded in 1984, Cisco stands as one of the largest multinational tech companies in the world. Its model has revolved around putting customers first and then establishing partnerships with those customers to identify their needs and offer solutions.

In addition, it offers hard products, solutions, software titles, and services to a wide array of customers and partners around the world. Its collaborators understand all the critical elements of everlasting success.

Cisco became the leader in networking and has transformed how people connect, communicate, and collaborate. If you ever hear the phrase "Welcome to the Human Network," think of Cisco, because they enable everyone to be connected!

Why It's a Web 3.0 Company

Business side:

- Like all the others, Cisco stays on the leading edge. As we speak, its programmers are building a smart and efficient energy grid.
- It has learned to adapt and capture new markets, called *market transitions*.
- Check out their list of product, service, and software lines—it's a mile long!
- They have a great partnership model. They know they need partners to succeed. They have thousands of partners and strategic alliances throughout the world.
- It is the worldwide leader in networking. Need I say more?

Marketing side:

- They regularly conduct virtual shows.
- They have a tool called My Cisco because they know engagement has always been a critical success factor. The My Cisco link lets you organize bookmarks, keep track of product and service announcements, support documents, and collaborate with the Cisco team, whether you're a new visitor or a long-time partner.

- Live video conferences are the norm.
- They use Twitter, forums, blogs, social networks, and beyond.
- Many of their products have virtual stores generating revenue.
- They are a major player in the mobile market.

There you have it: four of the most cutting-edge companies that understand innovation not only from a business sense, but also from a marketing sense. These companies were talking about Web 3.0 and the next wave before most of the competition. Watch their moves, and learn from their marketing. Even though they are huge companies, they still act quite entrepreneurial, so don't be discouraged if you are a small company, thinking, "What could I possibly learn from a billion-dollar business?" The answer: everything. They didn't begin as billion-dollar companies. Like the rest of us, the developers started with next to nothing and built an empire—and you can, too.

11

Your Action Plan: Putting It All Together and Taking Action

Now you're armed with all the tools to kick your marketing and business strategies up a notch. The final step is, of course, putting it all together.

What I've noticed after both attending and speaking at hundreds of conferences throughout the world is that people get very excited about the material, but a month or two later will be at the exact same place as they were they heard the new material. Don't let that happen to you.

To set a clear action plan and some goals, you need to know where you currently are (remember the 360-degree review you did in the beginning?), as well as where your competitors are. To do this, I'm going to use the ever-popular SWOT analysis. A SWOT analysis is a strategic approach to looking at the Strengths, Weaknesses, Opportunities, and Threats of a project, a business, or something of that nature. It is meant to help you quickly see things in a logical chart so you can plan accordingly. To make things easier to understand, I'm going to use a company I once owned as a case study.

To Do

How to Conduct a SWOT Analysis:

Step 1: *Grab a piece of paper and fold it in half.*

Fold in half again so you have four squares. You can also do this virtually, if you would like.

Step 2: *Label the four squares Strengths, Weaknesses, Opportunities, and Threats.*

Step 3: *List your thoughts and ideas about your marketing in the different columns.*

Make sure you don't leave anything out.

- **Strengths:** Where are things excelling? What are you good at? What's going well?

- **Weaknesses:** Where are things not going so well? What needs work?

- **Opportunities:** In what areas do you see potential growth? What areas should be explored?

- **Threats:** Where are the obstacles you may run into? What are the possible issues and areas to watch out for?

Here are some marketing-specific questions to ask yourself to better complete this activity:

- What Web 2.0 and 3.0 tactics are you using/ not using?

- What sites are you on/not on?

- Do you track everything?

- What type of analytical information are you getting back?

- How is the presentation of your materials?

- What feedback did you get from your customer surveys?

- What is the marketplace asking of you?

- How is your Web site?

- What type of interaction takes place in your marketing?

- How are you generating leads?

This list can go on forever. The idea is to ask the tough questions and then get real with the responses. You want a good mix of strengths, weaknesses, opportunities, and threats.

Case Study

Simply Soy, Inc., is a small, family-owned company that focuses on selling higher-end homemade soy candles and gift baskets. They started by selling solely through word of mouth and eventually expanded onto the Web. They quickly realized there were quite a few players on the Web already, and they would need to do things a bit differently to capture some market share. I recommended that they conduct a SWOT analysis before ramping up their Web marketing.

Simply Soy SWOT Analysis of Web Presence

Strengths:

- Pay-per-click going well

- Good reviews and feedback

- SEO is off to a great start

- Solid social networking

Weaknesses:

- Web site needs work; doesn't look professional

- Traffic is low

- Bounce rate is relatively high (not quality traffic)

- Branding

Opportunities:

- Start a blog

- Mobile play

- Additional products can be added

- Holiday themes seem popular

Threats:

- Major competition

- More and more companies popping up

- Many competing companies have much larger marketing budgets

- Economy issues

Using this information, they developed three-month and six-month SMART goals. SMART goals are goals that are **s**pecific, **m**easurable, **a**ttainable, **r**ealistic, and **t**imely. Keep reading as I go into much more detail about SMART goals.

The Result: The first thing Simply Soy accomplished was a total Web site redesign. After the site launched, they added a simple blog. Since mobile was a large opportunity, they released a mini Web site for browsing on a mobile phone.

On the strategy front, they shifted a bit to focus more on busy executives looking for gifts. This is where the mobile site really came in handy because these customers have a much larger likelihood of browsing the site on a mobile device. Using Google Analytics, the company's newly launched Web site went through numerous additional revisions to get the bounce rate (or the number of people who drop off the site very quickly) down to under 16%.

The company has seen a 350% increase in their bottom line year over year! They also released a new line of candles: "recession relief"!

Step 4: *Relax.*

After making a first pass at the strengths, weaknesses, opportunities, and threats, take a day and let the ideas sit.

Step 5: *Try again.*

Give the SWOT analysis one more pass and add any new items you might have come up with during that day of rest.

Step 6: Research the competition.

After you have your SWOT analysis complete, move on to your competitors. Research your top three to five competitors and perform the same SWOT analysis on them.

Obviously, you won't have insider information to know all their analytics and hard data, but there are plenty of free tools out there that will give you some good insight. www.Alexa.com is good for gathering basic analytical statistics for any site. It just takes a bit of investigating and some patience to find things on the Web.

Ask the same questions you asked before, but now about the competition. For example:

- How does their Web site look?

- What Web 2.0 and 3.0 tactics are they using?

- What are their customers or prospects saying?

- What data can be retrieved from sites like www.Alexa.com?

Step 7: *Get an objective perspective.*

Now that you have a SWOT analysis on your company, as well as a few competitors, have an outside party do a SWOT analysis on both your company and your competitors. Your analysis may be slightly skewed if you rely solely on your own judgment, either too critical or not critical enough. Locate your local SCORE chapter and take your information to them or post the project on a site like www.Guru.com or www.Elance.com for paid freelance help. Do not, however, show them your work. Their information needs to be fresh without any influence.

Step 8: *Set goals.*

Using this information, create your SMART goals for the next three to six months.

Your Action Plan for the Next Three to Six Months and Beyond

It's great to talk strategy and formulate ideas, but it's another thing to implement them. Don't get into analysis paralysis with these marketing ideas; formulate a clear plan of action.

I like to identify SMART goals and then follow up with three to five action items under each. I have been using SMART goals for years and it works best for me because there is little to be interpreted or misunderstood.

To Do

How to Set SMART Goals with Follow-Up Actions:

Step 1: *Make your SMART goals.*

To get you started, set no more than five SMART goals, because each goal is going to be followed up with action steps.

Example of a good SMART goal: Close $10,000 in new business by December 31.

Example of a poor SMART goal: Generate some new revenue soon.

Again, remember that SMART goals are specific, measurable, attainable, realistic, and timely. Only you will know if the goal is attainable, and the other attributes are easy to identify. Always have a timestamp on your SMART goals. How can you plan without any specific dates?

Step 2: *Make a list.*

Take each SMART goal and list three to five specific action steps that need to be accomplished to move you closer to that goal. What you will notice is that the action steps under each main SMART goal are also SMART goals themselves, in a way. It doesn't help if your SMART goals are great but your action steps aren't clear.

Since I talked about Simply Soy previously, let's use their SMART goals and the action steps needed to achieve each goal.

SMART goal #1: Design a new Web site for under $10,000 by January 15.

- Interview five design firms by October and hire the one that fits the job the best.

- Make a copy of the current Web site for backup purposes.

- Assign one staff member to a project-manager role to aid the design firm.

SMART goal #2: Launch a fully designed blog by September 15.

- Hire a WordPress expert to design the blog.

- Load content to the blog by September 1.

- Test the blog on different browsers and operating systems to ensure compatibility by September 10.

SMART goal #3: Design and launch a mobile Web site for under $3,000 by March 30.

- Engage a design and marketing firm that understands mobile by January 30.

- Have the same project manager on our side manage the mobile project to ensure completion on time and on budget.

- Solicit feedback from mobile customers to aid in the design process.

SMART goal #4: Perform SWOT analysis on the current market by September 30.

- Develop and send a customer survey using www.SurveyMonkey.com by September 1.

- Analyze the customer-survey feedback by September 10.

- Perform the SWOT analysis.

- Hopefully see where new markets are present from the previous data.

Step 3: *Revise and adjust your SMART goals, as needed.*

If the timelines or numbers need to change, do so as needed, but make sure you keep things in line with the SMART-goal formula.

Step 4: *Complete the action steps to make sure you hit the goals.*

Tas Tip

This is where 95% of people falter. They set the SMART goals but don't take any action steps to reach these goals. The minute you write down the action steps, make sure you initiate: Put things on your calendar, start soliciting résumés or bids for the different jobs, take action, and you will be ahead of 95% of entrepreneurs looking to reach the top! The old saying "90% of life is just showing up" needs a huge adjustment. Let's revise it to "90% of life is not just showing up, but taking clear and consistent action steps after you get there."

The Areas You Should Start with Immediately

I've discussed a lot of Web 3.0 marketing ideas in this book. It's up to you to pick and choose which ones can be easily adapted to fit your business. To help you, I wanted to identify the three areas you should focus on first. You have only so many hours in the day. Spend those hours on the three things covered next.

Video

I cannot stress video enough. Two years ago, it was fine to have a video camera and post some things from time to time. Today, consumers expect video sales pages, video testimonials, and video walk-ons (where you appear on your site with a welcome message). The companies that do not have video are being seen as inferior and outdated, and it is, quite frankly, costing them sales.

If you have not used video before, start small. Get yourself a Flip camera, and upload a few informational videos on www.YouTube.com. Don't be surprised or upset if they don't get 14 million views. Just get into the habit of shooting videos and posting them online.

After you get a bit more comfortable with the camera, post a video to your blog and solicit feedback. Chances are, you're going to get some great feedback and praise for the information. This will kick you up a notch to full-blown video shooting. Start shifting everything to video: testimonials, blogs, and descriptions. Give your audience lots to watch!

After you have done this (or if you're already an advanced videographer), conduct a video audit. Do you have videos on:

- All your sales pages?
- Your site as product descriptions?
- Your home page?
- Weekly (or daily) video blogs?
- YouTube?

Next, take your video up a notch by adding some walk-in or walk-out music. Either learn to do this editing yourself or hire a video expert. You can really jazz up videos!

Only after you have mastered static videos should you move on to live! Host a trial event on Ustream.TV and then a real one. If you get a bit more daring, keep a regular schedule for these live video events to acquire a consistent following.

Mobile

You read the numbers on cellphone usage, so don't ignore the mobile trend. Get a site that is mobile-friendly as soon as you can. If you're a service-based business, this is going to be relatively easy, because you need only a few pages. If you're product-based, make the site information-based, but also allow for people to purchase some of your more popular products right on the site. The reason I recommend putting only a few products on the mobile site is load time. Your potential buyers will get bored waiting for the site to load and will most likely click off.

After you have a mobile site in place, audit your mobile-marketing efforts. Are you asking for mobile numbers on all your sites, or are you still asking only for e-mail? Start collecting mobile numbers!

Finally, leverage the numbers, host contests, or try out an SMS or MMS campaign. Test the waters with a few different things and see what sticks. Not every mobile campaign will succeed, but I promise you that many will.

Mobile will rule the day in the very near future!

Collaboration Tools

Not only will the tools I presented help your marketing, but they will help your business in general. Go back through the chapter on collaboration and see what tools you can immediately start using. I'm confident that there are least a few you haven't adopted yet.

Get yourself on Google's platform—and you won't look back! After you have this down, make sure your customer relationship management system is helping your business rather than hurting it. If you don't have a CRM system, get one. (Again, I recommend www.Salesforce.com.)

Tas Tip

Virtual collaboration is the way business is being done today!

If you maintain an office with in-house staff, consider letting them work from home. My entire company is 100% virtual with contractors throughout the world. This one tip has helped save our clients millions of dollars every year. If you take my advice, send even 1% of the money you saved to one of my favorite charities, which you will read about in the next chapter, as a small "thank you."

Final Thoughts on the Evolution of the Web

The Web is changing constantly. Never stop reading and continuing your education. Stay on top of the current trends so that your business can constantly be ahead of that curve, leaving your competitors in the dust.

Here is how marketing trends will evolve in the near future:

- **Mobile:** More people in developing countries will be carrying mobile phones, with the vast majority carrying smartphones/PDAs.

- **Video:** Both cellphones and residential phones will have video conferencing available. Video quality will continue to improve and get easier for the ordinary person to not only shoot, but edit as well.

- **Blogging:** Blogging will continue to lose traction to microblogging sites and even more so to video, because it's just more entertaining than reading extensive text.

- **Searching:** The Web will continue to become more intelligent. This is all that semantic talk. Search engines will be better able to read your questions and give you better information.

- **Social networking:** Hundreds of thousands of smaller, more private social-networking sites will be popping up, many made by ordinary people with open-source technology.

- **Virtual reality worlds:** People will start getting over the fact that they think it's weird and start adopting it. www.SecondLife.com will become the new Facebook! In addition, virtual shows will continue to grab the market share from the live-event industry.

- **Workplace:** The general workplace structure will continue to get more informal and collaborative. Businesses will start allowing more employees to work from home and take advantage of the various Web-based collaboration tools. Flextime will become the norm, along with smaller teams.

- **The Web in general:** Everything and everyone will continue to move to the Web. Even the small businesses, from laundromats and pet groomers to plumbers and landscapers, will be on the Web. There is just no avoiding it. Businesses that don't adopt the shifts will suffer or close their doors.

The Web is and will continue to be the place to be!

Conclusion:
The Art of Giving Back

You might be wondering, *If this is a book on marketing, why end with a discussion on charity?* Now that I've given you my secrets, I want to ask something of you: Give back just 1% of the revenue this book helps you generate, and 1% of your time to some type of charity or social entrepreneurship cause. We're in a crazy time in the United States right now, like many other areas of the world. The worst thing we can do is scale back on our charitable works when times get tough.

I'll be very blunt with you: My passion is not for doing Internet marketing for others and making them rich. My passion is for enabling and educating others to use my techniques to make themselves rich. I'm able to reach a lot more people that way and change a lot more lives.

When I'm speaking, one of the most frequently asked questions I get is "Why did you become an entrepreneur versus anything else?" To me, there isn't really anything else that compares to being an entrepreneur, so I knew from a young age that it was what I wanted to become; but I've boiled down this answer to what I call the four Fs of why I love being an entrepreneur:

Fun: If you're not having fun, change what you're doing. I incorporate some fun into each and every day. You will learn that some of the most successful companies do this same thing. In fact, they foster and encourage it. Take Google, for example: They encourage you to take breaks in the PlayStation lounge, relax in the aquarium room in a massage chair watching the fish swim by, or even hustle to the massage room for a session of destressing with a hands-on masseur. Now that rocks!

Freedom: Running your own company allows you to enjoy much more flexibility than you might normally expect. Don't be surprised if you find yourself working on your patio, on a boat, or even sitting on the beach. With added freedom come choices. How do you want to spend your extra free time? I personally have declared Fridays to be family day. I'm also able to attend various meetings in my community and contribute my time and energy to various charities I endorse throughout the week.

Financial: I know it's tough to be an entrepreneur or even working as a marketing executive at a corporation in the beginning, but if you work intelligently, create your unique selling position, and use some of these marketing tactics, the financial end can become quite lucrative. As a marketer in a corporation, you will rewarded based on the success of the campaigns you help with or run. Money should not be the only reason you get into this game, but it sure has to be one of them.

Family: One of my all-time favorite books is by Jeffrey Gitomer, titled *Customer Satisfaction Is Worthless, Customer Loyalty Is Priceless*. The biggest takeaway I got from this book was when he said to take a picture of your family eating. Anytime you are on the brink of losing a customer or dealing with a dispute, look at the photo and realize that you're taking food out of your family's mouths if you handle the situation the wrong way. Yes, this seems very irrational, but think about it—it really is true. The customers are what's putting food on our tables, and we do what we do to love, support, and provide for our families.

One of the best ways I know how to make a difference is through charitable work. Everyone has a different definition of what charity means to him. For some, it's giving their time, for others it's solely money, and for some it's making a difference that will carry on for generations. Participating in any form of charity that feels right to you is what it's all about. To me, personally, it's a combination of everything. For some charities I simply give money, while others get my time and money, and for others I help in many random areas. You personally need to make the choices to give your time and money, not me. My only hope is that as your business grows and provides you more freedom, your giving gets bigger and more frequent!

As entrepreneurship continues to become more and more popular, various charities are popping up. One of the areas in particular is social entrepreneurship. A social entrepreneur recognizes a social problem or an area he or she can impact and uses entrepreneurial methods to create and manage a business or venture to make it happen. One of the first examples of social entrepreneurship is Ben & Jerry's Homemade Ice Cream. They realized they could make a big difference by donating money from every carton of ice cream sold.

Another great example of the social entrepreneur is Muhammad Yunus, founder of the Grameen Bank. This bank provides microloans to people looking to start their own businesses. In many cases, a loan for less than $50 for someone in a third-world country can allow them to start a thriving business that will supply them and many others with the resources they need for the rest of their lives. The risks are certainly evident, but to ensure repayment, the bank uses a system called "solidarity groups." These informal groups consist of several loan applicants who act as cosigners for one another. This builds not only a web of networking and business affiliates, but also one of trust, friendship, and community.

Since 1983 when the Grameen Bank was founded, Yunus and his foundation have loaned over $6.83 billion to more than 7.4 million borrowers. Many of the micolending groups also have record payback rates and some of the lowest default rates in the world.

Some of My Favorite Charities

In no way am I trying to influence you to give to any of these charities. I simply want to mention a few that I personally endorse.

St. Jude Children's Research Hospital

Web site: www.stjude.org

Many people are familiar with St. Jude's name, but I have found that few truly understand the impact this hospital has made on our nation and our world.

St. Jude is a premier pediatric hospital that focuses on treatment and in-house research for children stricken with cancer and other catastrophic diseases. Located in Memphis, Tennessee, the hospital's ultimate goal is to find a cure to heal these ailing children for life. The facility includes 2.5 million square feet of research, administrative offices, and clinical space dedicated to that particular goal.

The St. Jude doctors and staff have seen many of the nation's (and world's) sickest patients and most difficult cases, and are dedicated to the wellness of those children.

But with an operating cost of over $1.4 million per day, the hospital greatly relies on fundraising efforts to support its research and clinical productions.

I do not financially support St. Jude because they need my contribution, but because they deserve it. Here's why: All patients accepted for treatment at St. Jude are treated without regard to the family's ability to pay. A company (albeit, a hospital) willing to lend its services to the healing and well-being of ill children while running the risk of not being repaid? I'll contribute to that all day, every day. I have supported this charity since I was 16 years old, and I will continue to do so.

Make-a-Wish Foundation

Web site: www.wish.org

You are most likely familiar with this charity. They help numerous children living with life-threatening medical conditions achieve their wildest dreams.

The foundation's first official wish-child, 7-year-old Frank "Bopsy" Salazar, was granted his lifelong dream of becoming a firefighter. After a day of hosing down cars in his custom Phoenix Fire Department uniform, a ride in a hot-air balloon, and an entire day at Disneyland, Bopsy was presented his official wings as the city's first-ever honorary firefighter. Bopsy passed away after returning to the hospital from his Disneyland adventure, but he left this world having his greatest dreams fulfilled.

As of press time, 185,900 children like Bopsy have had their wildest wishes granted by the Make-a-Wish Foundation. Living with a terminal disease is difficult and emotionally draining for not only the ill child but his or her family as well. To see a big smile on such a small face is worth every dollar I could ever donate.

Women & Children's Hospital

Web site: www.wchob.org

This hospital is local to western New York, where I call home. It's rated as one of the best hospitals for children in the United States and is very, *very* close to my heart. My twin boys were born premature and had to be kept in the neonatal intensive care unit (NICU) in this very hospital. If you have been in a similar situation, you aren't surprised when I say it was one of the most challenging things my wife and I (and family) have ever experienced, seeing our precious little boys with tubes and wires running from every part of their bodies. It was a feeling of total helplessness. There were so many babies in the NICU, many who were much smaller than our boys. The same day our boys were admitted, another baby was admitted weighing less than one pound. Due to the constant care of the nurses and doctors, our twin boys are now healthier than ever.

Because I'm an entrepreneur, I was able to be there with my boys during the day and the evening. If I had been working a 9-to-5 job, that wouldn't have been the case. Because I was ever-grateful for the hospital, I wanted to give back in some way. When visiting my boys, I noticed that many of the other parents didn't have a place to sit to relax during the day while keeping an eye on their babies. Seven brand-new glider chairs and ottomans were donated in my sons' names (Connor Michael and Logan Michael) as just one small debt of gratitude paid to this hospital.

How to Start Giving Back

American Cancer Society: www.cancer.org

American Heart Association: www.americanheart.org

American Red Cross: www.redcross.org

AmeriCares: www.americares.org

Autism Speaks: www.autismspeaks.org

Big Brothers Big Sisters of America: www.bbbsa.org

Boy Scouts of America: www.scouting.org

Boys & Girls Clubs of America: www.bgca.org

Breast Cancer Research Foundation: www.bcrfcure.org

Cystic Fibrosis Foundation: www.cff.org

Feed the Children: www.feedthechildren.org

Food for the Poor: www.foodforthepoor.org

Girl Scouts of the USA: www.girlscouts.org

Goodwill Industries International: www.goodwill.org

Habitat for Humanity: www.habitat.org

Juvenile Diabetes Research Foundation International: www.jdrf.org

Kiwanis International: www.kiwanis.org

Lance Armstrong Foundation: www.livestrong.org

Leukemia & Lymphoma Society: www.leukemia-lymphoma.org

Lion's Club International Foundation: www.lionsclubs.org

March of Dimes Foundation: www.marchofdimes.com

Meals on Wheels Association of America: www.mowaa.org

Mothers Against Drunk Driving (MADD): www.madd.org

Muscular Dystrophy Association: www.mda.org

Ronald McDonald House Charities: www.rmhc.org

The Salvation Army: www.salvationarmyusa.org

Special Olympics: www.specialolympics.org

Susan G. Komen for the Cure: www.komen.org

United Way: www.liveunited.org

World Vision: www.worldvision.org

YMCA: www.ymca.net

YWCA: www.ywca.org

I trust that this tactical book on the latest and greatest Web 3.0 marketing trends will make a difference in your life, the lives of people around you, and the lives of those who are in much greater need than you may be.

Until we meet again,
From the heart,
Michael S. Tasner Jr.

Index

FINANCIAL TIMES

In an increasingly competitive world, it is quality of thinking that gives an edge—an idea that opens new doors, a technique that solves a problem, or an insight that simply helps make sense of it all.

We work with leading authors in the various arenas of business and finance to bring cutting-edge thinking and best-learning practices to a global market.

It is our goal to create world-class print publications and electronic products that give readers knowledge and understanding that can then be applied, whether studying or at work.

To find out more about our business products, you can visit us at www.ftpress.com.